OUR DISSERTATIONS, OURSELVES

OUR DISSERTATIONS, OURSELVES
SHARED STORIES OF WOMEN'S DISSERTATION JOURNEYS

Christine Sorrell Dinkins
and Jeanne Merkle Sorrell

OUR DISSERTATIONS, OURSELVES
Copyright © Christine Sorrell Dinkins and Jeanne Merkle Sorrell, 2014.

All rights reserved.

First published in 2014 by PALGRAVE MACMILLAN® in the United States—a division of St. Martin's Press LLC, 175 Fifth Avenue, New York, NY 10010.

Where this book is distributed in the UK, Europe and the rest of the world, this is by Palgrave Macmillan, a division of Macmillan Publishers Limited, registered in England, company number 785998, of Houndmills, Basingstoke, Hampshire RG21 6XS.

Palgrave Macmillan is the global academic imprint of the above companies and has companies and representatives throughout the world.

Palgrave® and Macmillan® are registered trademarks in the United States, the United Kingdom, Europe and other countries.

ISBN: 978-1-137-39523-8

Library of Congress Cataloging-in-Publication Data

Dinkins, Christine Sorrell.
  Our dissertations, ourselves : shared stories of women's dissertation journeys / Christine Sorrell Dinkins, Jeanne Merkle Sorrell.
    pages cm
  Includes bibliographical references and index.
  ISBN 978-1-137-39523-8 (pbk.)
  1. Doctor of philosophy degree. 2. Dissertations, Academic.
  3. Women—Education (Graduate) I. Sorrell, Jeanne Merkle.
  II. Title.
  LB2386.D56 2014
  378.2'4—dc23   2013034520

A catalogue record of the book is available from the British Library.

Design by SPi Global

First edition: February 2014

10 9 8 7 6 5 4 3 2 1

"It was a very long journey . . . But I think that is how it was for everybody . . . I mean, it's unbelievable to me what it was . . . On the other hand, I have to say, if I had it to do over again, I would."

— Naomi

To the inspiring women who shared stories of their doctoral journeys, inviting us to listen and to understand

Contents

Preface	ix
Acknowledgments	xiii
1 Writing the Unknown	1
2 Mystery, Confusion, Isolation	19
3 Realigning Relationships	47
4 Transformation of the Self	75
5 Advisor and Committee: Dancing with Strangers	103
6 End of a Journey and a New Beginning	139
7 Looking Back	161
Appendix: Gathering the Stories	179
Notes	191
Bibliography	195
Index	197

Preface

Because you live with your dissertation for several years, you embark on something you don't know. You have to work alone most of the time, you don't get as much feedback as you want to . . . you're by yourself in the libraries, nobody else knows what you're talking about. It's, it's a bizarre thing. I think you don't know what it is until you actually do it. It's a process that involves all your faculties. I think it involves your whole being.

— Louise

A dissertation is often a person's first major piece of independent research, and may be the largest and most complex writing project she has undertaken. Many students, including those who have been otherwise successful academically and professionally, do not finish their dissertation easily, take a longer time than expected to complete it, or do not complete it at all. Writing a doctoral dissertation can be an isolating experience. Peers in graduate school have their own goals and stress; friends and relatives may simply not understand the process. The dissertation advisor is often more of an authority figure than a sounding board or guide, and the dissertation can loom large even over gatherings that are supposed to offer a chance to relax and socialize.

The stories in this book suggest that even when dissertation writers feel that they are all alone, in a very important sense, they are not. Herein are gathered the stories of 20 women, ages 29–55, who at the time of their interviews had recently completed or were about to complete doctoral dissertations across a variety of disciplines: biology, English literature, modern languages, history, mathematics, music, nursing, philosophy, and social work. The voices of these women speak to common experiences, emotions, and challenges across disciplines, family situations, age, and background. Too often, stories like these stay private, because the people who live these stories have no one to share them with or fear no one will understand. The stories give voice to the incredible accomplishments, struggles, and personal journeys that happen to individual women in the dissertation process. As the authors of this book, we want to share these stories so that readers may see themselves in the stories and know they are not alone.

We are a mother and daughter, both of whom have written doctoral dissertations. Jeanne has a PhD in education and has worked as a researcher and professor of nursing. Christine, her daughter, has a PhD in philosophy and teaches philosophy and interdisciplinary courses. Christine had the immense good fortune to have her mother-mentor provide advice, encouragement, and the wisdom of personal experience throughout her dissertation process. We wanted to write this book because we both recognize the impact our respective dissertation processes had on us—the struggles, the strain, the newfound skills, and the eventual triumph that helped make us who we are today. And we wanted to write the book *together* because we believe in the power of shared inquiry and dialogue to bring to light themes, connections, and ideas that might otherwise be overlooked.

This book did not start out focused on *women* writing dissertations, but on men and women alike. We initially interviewed men and women and collected their stories about writing a dissertation. A research assistant who helped us early in the process, Lara Simpson Hrabota, pointed out that a pattern had begun to emerge. Men and women had, by and large, strikingly different concerns, experiences, frustrations, and transformations during and after the dissertation process. For example, many of the women struggled with balancing their roles as mothers with the time their dissertation work demanded. Women also seemed more troubled and even disoriented by a lack of communication or solid relationship with their advisors. In looking back on their dissertation experience after completion, many of the women also commented on the change and growth of personal relationships, whereas the men observed little of this change.

In this book, we do not attempt to differentiate between the dissertation experiences of men and women, nor do we wish to persuade the reader that women's dissertation experiences are essentially different than men's. Rather, we focus on commonalities among the women's experiences, attempting to convey a coherent picture to readers while presenting variations within that picture in an honest way. Some of these experiences may also be shared by men, but from listening intently to our participants' stories, we believe there is a common thread that makes these stories *women's* stories. Thus, we decided to write this book about, and largely for, women dissertators. We believe, however, that male graduate students and female and male dissertation advisors will also learn from the similarities and differences in these women's experiences.

The women we interviewed talked about how they sought out dissertating friends to share their stories of the dissertation experience, laughing and sometimes crying together in order to move beyond the isolation imposed upon them by the dissertation. Following that same instinct and desire, this book seeks to share these women's stories with readers so that the readers might see themselves and their experiences as part of a shared narrative. The philosopher Alasdair MacIntyre characterizes humans as "storytelling animals" who understand their own lives and possibilities through the stories they hear and tell.[1] Each of us sees her own possibilities outlined in the stories she grows up with, and each of us sees her life as a narrative in which she is the main subject. Thus, the telling and sharing of stories is a way for all of us to understand our own experiences and possibilities.

In addition to its primary mission of sharing stories, this book is also a qualitative research study and thus provides readers an opportunity to experience qualitative research in a personal way. Details of our research methodology can be found in the Appendix. In giving voice to these women's stories, we presented interview data as direct quotes from our participants. For the most part, we have limited our interpretations of their stories to a *Reflections* section at the end of each chapter, wishing to let the stories speak for themselves.

In Barry Lopez's book, *Crow and Weasel*, Badger tells Crow: "If stories come to you, care for them. And learn to give them away where they are needed. Sometimes a person needs a story more than food to stay alive. That is why we put these stories in each other's memories. This is how people care for themselves."[2] We hope that this book will be read by women writing dissertations so that they may garner support, perspective, insight, inspiration, and guidance from detailed stories of the struggles and successes of twenty women who also tread through this territory that was as new and strange for them as it is for our readers. We also hope it will be read by partners and friends who wish to understand better the process that the women in their lives are going through. And we most dearly hope that dissertation advisors will read this book to gain insights into the thoughts, fears, and hopes of women graduate students as they face this most difficult part of the journey to their doctoral degrees.

We now hand our readers over to the twenty women who will share their stories: Alecia, Audrey, Bubbles, Callie, Celeste, Claire, Eleanor, Gabriella, Greta, Gretchen, Joanne, Kate, Kim, Louise, Martha, Mary, Monique, Naomi, Stella, and Suzy.

Acknowledgments

We gratefully acknowledge the many persons who have contributed to the completion of this book. We cannot possibly list all of these special individuals but would like to acknowledge the following: Lara Simpson Hrabota, who suggested we devote this book to women's stories; Pat Black, Kim Cox, Judy English, Tagwa Omer, and Mon Sookratree for their generous assistance with our research during their own doctoral studies; the Wofford Writers Group, for their constant encouragement and motivation; our wise and patient husbands, Christopher Dinkins and Gregory Sorrell, for their always-ready support; our women participants, who trusted us to share their stories of struggles and success; and each other, for the mentoring that goes between mother and daughter, daughter and mother, as our lives and learning overlap.

Christine Sorrell Dinkins and Jeanne Merkle Sorrell

Chapter 1

Writing the Unknown

> *When you start you think, oh, I'm going to answer an enormous question and make such a difference. But that's just not true. You're going to answer maybe a part of a question, or you're going to add to the body of knowledge about a question that others are working on. But that kept me up at night, you know?*
>
> — Mary

Anyone who enters a doctoral program knows that something called "the dissertation" looms at the end of the program of studies. She may look forward to this project as the culmination of her scholarly work, she may dread it, or she may have no idea what it actually *is*. The stories we gathered revealed a wide difference in perceptions about what a dissertation means. When asked to define the term dissertation, some of the women we interviewed expressed preconceptions about what it is, some were unsure, and some seemed entirely stumped at trying to define it. In spite of the fact that faculty advisors use the term dissertation as if everyone knows what it is, these women's perceptions differed widely, and some, even after completing the dissertation, were still not sure if they had completed the dissertation correctly.

Thus, the question arises: If a person does not know what a dissertation is, how can she write one?

The Stories

For some of the women we interviewed, the fact that the dissertation was original and their own was the overriding quality to strive for. Other women talked matter-of-factly about how the dissertation was a demonstration of their capability to tie together their previous course work in this culminating project; the originality and ownership of their work was not as important as being able to demonstrate their competency in understanding the important research in their discipline. Finally, for some women, the dissertation represented simply an intellectual exercise—a hoop that they needed to jump through in order to get the doctoral degree.

A Project of One's Own

Participants sometimes responded to the question "What is a dissertation?" as "Something original." These women held the originality of the work as paramount. When Stella reflected back on the time that she was beginning her dissertation, she remembered that she really had only a vague idea what a dissertation was, but the thing that stood out for her was that it needed to be original:

It was the first piece of writing I did that was completely mine—my perspective and way of explaining a topic that I had researched very intensely and had come to original conclusions on that furthered the understanding of the topic . . . And I think, before, I thought a dissertation is something you write and defend, obviously, but umm . . . something you write that is original research, meaning it's doing something that wasn't done before. And in my case, I do think that's true, but I just had a different vision of it, I didn't expect it to be quite so wholly mine. I didn't expect that . . . I didn't quite know what it meant to contribute to a scientific field,

I think. And I think that . . . like at the very beginning, it seemed like a very overwhelming and daunting task, because I didn't really know what it meant to do original research.

Eleanor also had only a vague idea what a dissertation was but sensed that she needed to find her own definition. She expressed it this way:

When I started thinking about the question, I had trouble separating it from what I believe other people think it should be . . . and it's kind of funny because one of the things I think a dissertation is means our making that separation, and figuring out what we really do believe. But I think if I were going to describe it, it's coming up with an idea that's unique, beginning to form an argument for how to support that idea and seeing what follows from it, doing extensive research, not only around the idea but also around the implications, and then coming up with a way to identify again, after doing all that, what the idea really is, and to be able to express it and state it, and identify and defend it against helpful objections . . . If it's not a unique idea, then you're not forced to go through some of those steps of actually asserting something, backing it, as something that you truly believe, and not just something that's a theory. Also, if it's unique, you have to have gone through a certain process to arrive at it, and that if it's the right process, I like to think it involves some sort of moral stance, you've made a commitment to discovery, exploration, also a commitment to what ideas mean, that they should have value, that they shouldn't just be something that could be obtained already, that it's not just an exercise, so the uniqueness would also hopefully involve that kind of commitment.

Eleanor's comment demonstrates the temptation to think of the dissertation in terms of what others believe it to be. Yet, it was the personal definition of this term that we wanted to elicit from the women we interviewed. When Eleanor did press herself for her own definition, she emphasized presenting a unique idea and tied that closely with a sense of personal ownership in articulating and defending this original idea.

Alecia also emphasized the original nature of the dissertation, comparing the writing of a dissertation to pregnancy:

> The whole idea is very pregnancy-like, it's very much your baby that you create, but it would be like if I had the power to pull sperm off a shelf and put it in me, 'cause it's totally you and I guess what people are able to do is to say, okay, this is my genes, and I want this, this, this, this, and this. Okay, let's find somebody to put the other pieces of this, this, this, this, and this. I just think it's so much so the overwhelming part of doing something that nobody else has done . . . and having this huge project that looms ahead of you, that you've spent all this time working in this area, developing this thing, you have some definite ideas about how this is, and then you're creating this kinda baby of yours.

Monique expressed a similar sense of personal ownership when she talked about how she perceived her doctoral dissertation as different from her master's thesis:

> [For the master's thesis] I did end up with a written document reflecting the pieces but it was different from the dissertation. Because the dissertation, from start to finish—it was all mine. At the master's level, while it was mostly mine, I guess I had a little more help maybe from the faculty in terms of how to sort of put it together. But with the dissertation . . . it was from beginning to end how you wanted to create it, develop it; you had the faculty to bounce things off of, you know, in terms of ideas. But it's yours—totally yours—in terms of its creation and how it's all put together. So, in terms of the thesis, that's how I see the dissertation being different. It is more comprehensive—you are really involved in it from the beginning to the end . . . There is something kind of exciting about getting down and being able to express for others what is really important to them. About the certain phenomenon that you are going to be examining.

Monique's emphasis on personal ownership was expressed by Callie as "authenticity." Callie reflected deeply on her personal relationship with the dissertation process, noting that it felt like she was moving into a completely different realm of understanding, which she described as a huge learning curve. Her research focused on women, and she saw the purpose of the dissertation as representing authentically the women that were involved in her study. She also thought about how the development of the dissertation had affected her own development. She was passionate about her dissertation topic and was clear in her need to keep the women in the study very central and make sure their voices were heard throughout this process. She said:

> I think probably for me, this dissertation . . . it's about representing authentically the women that are involved . . . I have to keep them very central and make sure their voices are heard throughout this process . . . It's such a reflective process to go through, and always constantly to check where I am, you know. And where I'm going. The women are telling me things that they've never told anybody apart from maybe their significant other. And then you do feel an awful sense of responsibility, that you don't want that to be for nothing. And you want to honor that as best as you can . . . I think it is a huge journey, and it's affected me an awful lot more than I thought it would . . . Just so that *I* feel proud of it.

Trying to write a document that is original, unique, and authentic, and also makes the writer proud, is certainly an intimidating task for someone who is likely a novice in scholarly writing. The thought of the dissertation needing to meet these criteria seemed to paralyze the writing process for some women as they wondered how they could accomplish such goals. Mary laughed as she described the circularity of her thoughts in thinking about the dissertation:

> *If* I had an original question—I mean, I don't know if there is an original question, but at least going through and proving that, if I had thought of an original question, that I know how to go about finding out the answer . . .

As the women reflected on what the dissertation meant to them, they seemed to enjoy thinking about how their ideas had changed since they began the process. Mary laughed when she thought about how she had initially viewed the dissertation:

> When you start you think, oh, I'm going to answer an enormous question and make such a difference. But that's just not true. You're going to answer maybe a part of a question, or you're going to add to the body of knowledge about a question that others are working on. But that kept me up at night, you know?

As Eleanor described her ideas, it was evident that for her too, just thinking about the importance of the originality aspect of the dissertation left her bewildered:

> If it is an original idea you came up with, then that means people won't necessarily have said a lot about the idea itself, they might have said a lot about side issues or implications or things surrounding it. So, to actually begin working with the idea again, not only is it the case that you don't want to get lost in the side points, you have to kind of have the nerve to assert your idea and discuss it when it might . . . and this is where it starts to get lost in what other people might think. It always seems to me that, in the back of people's minds, they feel, well, if it's legitimate it's already been discussed in some way. So if you're discussing something that's completely new, then you're going to need to be putting forward arguments that haven't been put forward yet, and you're not going to have the things to back it up that we're used to when we write smaller kinds of papers.

It appeared from many of the interviews that this quality of originality was a new and intimidating characteristic of the research and writing for these women. Of course, all of their previous scholarly papers had been expected to be original in that they used references to support ideas that were supposed to be their own, not those of other scholars. But the dissertation presented a much bigger challenge to integrate their original ideas with scholars before them. And in some ways, it seemed also to be the first time the women thought of themselves as scholars. Not knowing how to implement the role, they sometimes felt like impostors who had no business constructing and taking sole ownership of such a project.

Demonstration of Required Knowledge

Some women we interviewed saw the dissertation most importantly as the means to demonstrate that they had learned enough through their program of studies to make them capable of scholarly research. They did not focus on originality and ownership as much as the need for competency in the research and writing. They had entered a doctoral program, knew that they would need to write a dissertation at the end of their studies, and accepted that as part of the requirements for the degree they sought.

Suzy was matter-of-fact in her description of how she saw the dissertation when she started it; it was more about what she needed to demonstrate for someone else than it was about being a project of her own:

> As I was going through it, I remember thinking, this is just a giant student project (laughs). It's so structured and yet there's so much guidance with an advisor always. You need to do this, do that, so much suggestion, this is what you need to do, that won't work. Of course, it's a requirement for graduation, for getting a PhD. A giant student project. Yes, I knew I was in the research world, so to speak, but it always felt like another big assignment, is how I pictured it. Not research on your own. Everything that it entailed, the learning that goes along with that kind of assignment, the investigation, all that kind of thing. It was very different because it was all-encompassing, all the things you learn in class and all your life experience went into this . . . It really became the end-all, be-all student project, as opposed to research projects I've worked on before. This was the big project . . . But it's a student thing, you do this so you learn. So I approached the dissertation with the same mentality. This is more writing than you will ever have to do as a practicing researcher but you do it now because this is how you learn.

Even while focusing on the process of writing her dissertation so that she would meet the "this is what you do" requirements of her advisor, Suzy did worry about losing her own voice in the process:

> *Suzy:* It's painstaking because sometimes it's hard to find your voice within the standard methodology.
> *Researcher:* That's interesting, what do you mean by finding your voice?
> *Suzy:* You need to find where you personally fit in to a very organized and very structured methodology of finding the answer to your question . . . to find where the half point is between your expertise in your field and how it works into that scientific methodology, into that scientific structure and I think you find, or at least I did, you find where you can go with that, like—wow, I can use this structure, I didn't think I could. I didn't know what I would do with it.

Some women did not appear to have thought deeply about what the process meant for them beyond a proof of knowledge and competence, or how writing a dissertation would help them grow intellectually as a researcher. When asked to define a dissertation, Monique saw it simply as showing what she had learned, though she had a very positive attitude toward that idea of the dissertation:

That is the time you want to show what it is you have learned, what it is you have discovered in the process of doing this research—that can be pretty exciting.

Kim also saw the process of demonstrating competency as paramount:

For me, it was just the process—describing a program of research, a researchable idea that had passed scientific examination, and the process of writing up those results. I think it was . . . the rationale for the researchable idea, the technique or testing you use to find the answer to that research question, the statistics that back up the findings, and then the implications of the findings to the broader world.

Kim's choice of the phrase "writing up the results" appears to reflect the views of many of the women we interviewed. It seems to convey that the writing up of the results is the most important part of the dissertation process in their minds—not the growth as a researcher and scholar.

Gabriella also defined a dissertation in terms of the demonstration of what she had learned in the doctoral program and did not seem to think about the importance of carrying out the dissertation process so that it would provide the intellectual growth that she needed to launch a career in research:

> The dissertation is a research project that culminates a doctoral program and that is meant to tie together things that you learned through the program, but also the results of the research you did as a student and that is usually the last requirement of the doctoral program before you launch out into a career, often to continue in that area of research.

Kate had similar thoughts as she talked about the dissertation process:

> I think of it as a very long, drawn-out process that probably started with the very first class I had [in the doctoral program]. In thinking about what topic of research was of interest to me, and how I might actually design a study to evaluate a certain hypothesis or question, I went through a long and lengthy process of designing and implementing and collecting data. And then, ultimately, writing the dissertation up. Then you still have to defend it, then it gets published, so it takes many years, and it's a very long part of your life.

Gretchen's comments suggested that she saw the benefits of the dissertation in that the degree gave her the credibility—with regard to research—that she needed in order to have "a level playing field" with peers at her career level in the university, but she was vague in exactly how it would help her achieve the expertise she would need:

> When I hear the word "dissertation," I think research degree. So the end product is this big research project that prepares you to

go and do more research in your career. And the other thing I was thinking . . . "lengthy" is the other word that comes to mind . . . *big*. [The dissertation] gives you a great deal of credibility with regard to research. I mean, it is a research degree. It creates a level playing field when I go and meet with other deans and directors. I have the same credentials. It also, because of that, that reasoning, that thought process and critical reasoning, that takes you to a higher level that I think of as necessary for this type of position, [makes you] sort of have to think about the steps that other people haven't thought about or step back to look at the big picture . . . "Expert" comes to mind, because you know, before I got into the dissertation I had other education that required studying research, for doing research projects and so I felt prepared going into the doctoral program. And so, by the time you get finished with the dissertation, you may not be an expert in that particular research field or in that field of study, but you should be able to go out and do more research, because you've got the research degree.

The stories of Suzy, Monique, Kim, Gabriella, Kate, and Gretchen reflected those of many of the women who trusted that the universities had set up the requirement of a dissertation for a good reason, and thus they would meet that requirement with their best efforts. They did not seem to think much further about what they should gain from the process. In contrast, Martha was able to reflect on that perspective from her past roles as both a student and a faculty member. At the time of her interview, she was a faculty member and saw the dissertation differently than she had when she was a student. Her description of the changes in her perceptions illustrates important differences between student and faculty perspectives:

Before I actually got involved in the academic setting, there wasn't a whole lot of clarity on what [the dissertation] meant. The way that it was described to me and the reason for the dissertation is that it's an opportunity for you to demonstrate what you have learned over the course of your studies and taking a particular question that is of interest to you. It may not be your life's work, but it is of interest to you, and [provides an] opportunity to explore that question while demonstrating to the faculty and your committee and others that you have been able to grasp the concepts that are involved in research and then apply that in a manner that makes sense to you and then may be of use to you in your later career. So that's kind of . . . what a dissertation meant to me while I was in the midst of it, while I was a doctoral student.

And now I think I continue to feel that way very strongly, but also that it kind of sets the individual up as they continue their research career, because it sets them up in a research opportunity for them to look at things not only on a research level, but on a practical application level. And also, it's the opportunity for them to hone their written communications skills. Because as I see it as a doctoral faculty member now, that's probably the most difficult thing that I see students struggle with. It's their ability to put their ideas into writing in an organized way. Because it takes them a while. All of them, the dissertation allows the individuals to apply their knowledge in an area that is of particular interest to them, it enables them to develop the critical thinking skills to figure out, what difference does my question make? You know, is it meaningful to anybody other than me? Can they take that and express it in a written communication in a way so that the knowledge that comes from their study can then be enjoyed by others?

These women students saw the dissertation as a vehicle to demonstrate that they were competent in implementing a research project and "writing it up" in a manner that would meet the expectations of their doctoral committee and the university requirements for the doctoral degree. They took pride in their accomplishment—that they had met this goal.

Just a Hoop!

For some women, the dissertation did not represent the path to future research that faculty no doubt envisioned for their students, but rather "an exercise," a "rite of passage," or "a hoop to jump through." Louise laughed as she shared her perceptions of what a dissertation is, even after completing it:

I still don't know. I think it's an exercise. It was a process, it was an intellectual exercise and also a—I don't want to say, but a psychological [exercise]—it's something that you go through . . . You write something and you have to rewrite it and rewrite it, and who knows who will read it, apart from your jury? And then you wonder why you did this! At this point, this is where I am. And I did it because it gives me a degree, and it gives me a decent paycheck.

Alecia saw the demonstration of knowledge as itself a rite of passage:

It's your chance to prove what you've learned and kind of demonstrate what you've learned. So, it's a huge return demonstration of the knowledge that you've gotten, and showing people that you can put together some project . . . a rite of passage.

Greta shared similar thoughts:

The dissertation means that it's the final product. It shows that you've completed your doctoral coursework, and so you don't get your diploma until you've finished the dissertation. So I guess it's an artifact of completion (laughs). It's a nice bound little book that I have in my library that I shared with other people that helped me along the way . . . because there were so many things that I wanted and needed to do. I became realistic that the doctoral program is, you know—once you finish your classes and the dissertation—it's just starting. And so it doesn't have to be your best piece. The best part about it is that it's done . . . Maybe, probably, part of that story is my mother finished everything but her master's thesis and had children and never finished. So . . . "done" was important.

Claire put the same ideas more bluntly:

I just wanted to be done with the stupid thing. I couldn't tell that I was learning anything from the process, and I certainly didn't think anyone outside my committee was going to read this thing I was pouring all my time and energy into. The only thought that got me through was knowing that this was what was standing between me and being a college professor.

Naomi had not done anything with the data since finishing her dissertation and saw it as merely a hoop to jump through to attain her goal of a doctoral degree:

I think of it as an academic exercise, it's a hoop that you have to jump through, it's a way of proving that you know what you're talking about, that you can actually do research at the PhD level . . . but I just think "get it done!" . . . It was my experience, and the experience of the students in my program for my PhD . . . that, by the time you were able to meet all of your committee's requirements for the dissertation, it was going to be extremely long. Almost like a "badge of honor" kind of thing? The thing you had to do. And it had to be very complete, very thorough. For actually sort of starting out my research program, I would say it was completely useless . . . I kinda looked at it as a hazing thing or a rite of passage. And I wasn't very happy about it, but it didn't seem like there was much that you could really argue . . . They wanted even more lit review on mine, which didn't seem appropriate, since mine was three published papers. It seemed ridiculous to do a thorough lit review on top of it when I already had done three separate lit reviews on my papers. And my advisor's response was, "Well, that's just what a dissertation is." . . . I truly look at it as a hoop that I needed to jump through in order to graduate . . . And my overriding feeling, especially now that I'm an advisor to PhD students, is "the best dissertation is a *done* dissertation!"

Naomi also recognized in her own experience the tension between differing student and faculty perceptions of what a dissertation means. For that reason, she initiated a survey at her school to try to determine a better definition of a dissertation:

I actually polled our graduate school about what a dissertation would consist of, and . . . it was pretty, relatively vague—nothing about the length. Mostly it had to do with the content . . . but they left it vague enough that the committee could make it almost anything that they wanted to.

It was clear that most of the women, even if they emphasized the requirement of originality or demonstration of required knowledge, did see the dissertation as a means to an end. As described by Celeste, who was still dissertating at the time of her interview:

I have thought about that, and what it is for me, is a means to an end. I'm trying to research something that will help me in my teaching and my students in their learning. So it's a topic, you know, and it's a paper done through research, that will help improve my teaching.

When asked if she would have defined it that way before starting the dissertation, she responded:

No. My idea of it has changed. I thought it would be just anything that interested you, or that you felt like you had to do or were assigned to do, or something like that, but as I started even developing the title and doing the proposal, it evolved into "Well that won't help me as much as if I do so-and-so." So you know, I just tried to focus it so that it would be helpful to me or to my courses.

Joanne also saw the dissertation as checking off a box, but she looked ahead to her further research work that would come after the dissertation. She said:

The dissertation is only a step in the process. For this whole thing to make any difference to anybody—nobody reads the dissertation, very few people read the dissertation. And so the dissertation helps you check the box. And that was really the frame of reference, that this dissertation was a means to an end. It wasn't the end—it was going to be the articles that came from the dissertation that was the important piece. I had to get the box checked in order to get my degree, but the dissertation wasn't the stopping point.

Unlike Joanne, the voices of Louise, Alecia, Greta, Claire, Naomi, and Celeste indicate that, for them, the dissertation was a vehicle to move them forward, in that they would have the doctoral degree that would open new career opportunities for them, but the dissertation itself was not necessarily seen as something that would set them on a new research journey. The focus was on getting something necessary completed. Naomi is now a faculty member and discusses with her students her definition of the dissertation as a hoop to jump through.

Reflections on the Stories

As noted in the preface, Louise said, "You don't know what it is until you actually do it." Many women in our study talked about the vagueness of what a dissertation meant to them. This is quite the Catch-22. If one does not know what a dissertation is, how can she write one? As we listened to the women struggle with trying to articulate a personal definition of a dissertation, it reminded us of Alice's conversation with the Cheshire Cat in Lewis Carroll's *Alice's Adventures in Wonderland*. It was almost as if we could substitute the faculty advisor's identity with that of the Cheshire Cat:

> *Alice:* Would you tell me, please, which way I ought to go from here?
> *Cat:* That depends a good deal on where you want to get to.
> *Alice:* I don't much care where.
> *Cat:* Then it doesn't much matter which way you go.
> *Alice:* . . . so long as I get somewhere.
> *Cat:* Oh, you're sure to do that, if only you walk long enough.[1]

This uncertainty expressed by Alice and the women in this chapter is similar to the challenge posed to Socrates by his friend Meno: "How will you look for [something], Socrates, when you do not know at all what it is? How will you aim to search for something you do not know at all? If you should meet with it, how will you know that this is the thing that you did not know?"[2] Socrates responds to this very troubling puzzle—one that could be a threat to all inquiry—by asserting his belief that we all have truths already in us that we can find through reflection. Even if that is not the case, he argues, he is certain that "we will all be better people, wiser and more able, if we search for the things we do not know."[3] In another similar exchange, Socrates expresses his confidence that those who search, even when they do not know where they are going, "discover within themselves a multitude of beautiful things, which they bring forth into the light."[4]

Socrates' answer to this paradox may explain how students do, in fact, successfully complete the dissertation even when they do not know what it is supposed to be. But that does not prevent the vagueness of the goal from being stressful or even frightening. Should faculty therefore be more prescriptive in telling doctoral students what a dissertation should be? Probably most faculty would agree with Eleanor, Monique, Callie, and Mary that the dissertation should represent originality and authenticity and should promote a sense of personal ownership in the ideas and conclusions. But those ideas are hardly enough to convey a thorough sense of what a dissertation is meant to be.

It is probably less important for a faculty advisor to provide a specific definition for a dissertation than it is for the student to reflect on what it means to her. Such a process of reflection can help the writer find the sense of ownership she may be seeking and help her find meaning in the dissertation for her own personal growth as a scholar, so that the dissertation can truly become more than just a hoop. Such reflection can also help a writer recognize some of the freedom that is hers to decide on her own definition; this freedom may be frightening, but it can also be quite empowering.

There will always be differing definitions of a dissertation among doctoral students and faculty. This difference can create tension between a faculty dissertation advisor and the doctoral student, but perhaps this tension is not necessarily bad. If one purpose of a dissertation is to build scholarly understanding, it is possible that the dissertation process can be used in part as a fruitful avenue for exploring perceptions of what a dissertation is, or what it means to create a significant scholarly work of a certain scope. If the tension between differing perceptions of students and faculty seems to be impeding student progress, it is reasonable for a student to initiate a dialogue with her faculty advisor to share perceptions, make her own informed decision about what the dissertation will be, and agree with her advisor on a clear path for what is to be accomplished with the dissertation. Even if the student and advisor cannot achieve mutual agreement on the definition for the dissertation, it is important for the student to at least have a better idea than Carroll's Alice did of where she wants to go, so she can work with the advisor to get there.

We found in our interviews that when students did seek guidance as to the expected nature of the dissertation, often faculty would give them copies of completed dissertations to review, as if just seeing the nice bound book would help the students understand what they had to do. Instead, the result from such an attempt to help seemed more likely to lead to intimidation and uncertainty, since each dissertation is unique, and a student is unlikely to understand what *her* dissertation is supposed to be simply by seeing someone else's.

As the women in our study struggled with defining the dissertation, the ideas became clearer to them as they shared their stories with us. Few of the women in our study had the experience of sharing their stories before speaking with us. Just as we have approached this book as shared inquiry to help our participants and ourselves better understand the beliefs and assumptions relevant to the inquiry, it is likely that women currently working on dissertations would benefit from even informal shared inquiry on questions such as "What is a dissertation?" A conversation with a peer over coffee or a frank conversation with one's advisor could do a world of good not just in gathering ideas from others but in helping the dissertator understand and explore her own ideas and beliefs.

Even with such a wide variety of perceptions and definitions among our participants, all the stories are valid. We cannot say that the views of the women who saw the dissertation as merely a hoop to jump through were somehow less accurate than the views of those who believed that the essence of the dissertation was originality. In fact, some of the women who viewed the dissertation as a necessary hurdle but not a great piece of original research have gone on to very successful careers in academia with impressive publication records. Thus, perhaps it is not only unrealistic to have one single definition of a dissertation, it may also be unnecessarily restrictive. If the dissertation process is expected to help a student toward a future role as researcher and scholar, certainly there are many different paths to that goal.

Readers struggling to define a dissertation or to understand their own goals in writing one may wish to engage in shared inquiry and informal dialogue among peers and faculty. They will likely find it helpful to ask themselves and others: What is a dissertation? What do I want it to be, for me? Is it a hoop? Is it demonstration of what I have learned? How important is originality to me and my advisor, and what does originality mean in this context? How do I make this project my own while still fitting it within the parameters set out by my advisor and program?

Reflecting on questions like these can help to shed light on writing the unknown and build scholarly understandings among both students and faculty.

Chapter 2

Mystery, Confusion, Isolation

I'm just seeing all the branches and not seeing what it is that holds them up. I don't know how else to put it.

— Eleanor

One of the biggest challenges in the dissertation process is simply the mystery of it all. As we saw in Chapter 1, doctoral students struggle with defining what a dissertation is supposed to be in the first place. That difficulty in defining a dissertation leads in turn to the emotions and frustration the women are giving voice to in this chapter. Since, in almost all cases, a dissertation is the first project of such scope for the writer, previous experience may not be sufficient to overcome obstacles. The how-to and self-help books available may not necessarily help enough, either; perhaps they even contribute to the mystery, confusion, and isolation voiced in this chapter. As Mary said:

I read five books on . . . not theory books, practical pragmatic books on how to survive a dissertation. Okay, I read five of them, and I was reading them about a year before I finished my coursework . . . And I had a different experience than a lot of the books.

Celeste had a similar disillusionment with these how-to books:

> I don't feel like I was warned . . . You know they have these books out that say finish your dissertation in 24 months—really ridiculous stuff out there—and there's really nothing that says it's going to kick your butt. So you know that's not out there. And it'll just kick your butt. It just does.

These advice books tend to be one-size-fits-all, and they can leave doctoral students feeling as lost in the mystery as ever, as each finds that her own experience fails to fit the parameters or assumptions of the books. Our hope is that this book of stories from a variety of women will have the opposite effect.

Another reason there seems to be so much mystery and confusion surrounding the dissertation process is that nearly everyone who does it, does it only once. As Martha pointed out:

> You know, I think anybody that teaches any kind of class about the dissertation, we all kinda realize what our limitations are, and that we've all done that exactly once. If I speak to a group of students about how to write a dissertation, you know I've done it just one time myself. You know, nobody really has . . . except if somebody has a dual degree. But most people have only written one dissertation. So here I am saying, okay, I'm taking my experience, which is a grand total of one.

If each dissertation advisor and committee member has only gone through the dissertation process once as a student, and each process is unique to that individual, is it any wonder that graduate students find they have trouble navigating the mysterious, confusing, and isolating process of writing a dissertation?

The Stories

As we spoke with the women about some of the more difficult times in their dissertation-writing experience, what we heard most frequently was the overwhelming and seemingly inescapable mystery of the whole process. With little relevant experience and, often, little guidance, each dissertation writer is expected to find her own unique path to complete a project whose very nature she may barely understand. In turn, this lack of experience and guidance can lead to frustration and confusion or even periods of being stuck or overcome by writer's block. Along with such frustrations, a dissertation writer may also battle feelings of isolation as she finds that those around her do not understand her struggles or simply cannot help.

While the combined factors of mystery, confusion, and isolation can be incredibly difficult for some dissertation writers, these factors can also have a positive effect on the scholar, as we will see at the end of this chapter. The personal and intellectual growth and confidence that come from struggling with these factors can perhaps make this difficult journey worthwhile.

The Mystery

Many of the women we spoke with expressed a feeling of mystery about the entire dissertation process—a sense of mystery caused by several factors. Some women found themselves going simultaneously in different directions as they faced the initial phase of choosing a topic. Other women felt that the process and steps involved in completing the dissertation were not well defined nor communicated in a clear and timely manner. Some found that transitioning from the kind of writing they had done for their coursework to the kind of writing required for the dissertation constituted a large and frightening leap into the unknown. Still others struggled with the change in the nature and timing of feedback on their research and writing compared to what they had experienced during the rest of their graduate education.

Choosing a topic for a dissertation can seem like a daunting task because the dissertator knows that in choosing a topic, she is choosing a direction for her research for the next few years; in fact, she may even feel that she is choosing a path for her life for years to come. The overwhelming options in picking a topic can cause bewilderment as to how even to start the dissertation project. Mary explained:

The whole first part of the process, which probably took three years for me, was figuring out what area and what question I was interested in finding out an answer to.

Gabriella also struggled with choosing a topic, and her comments illustrate how a student might feel pulled in different directions even as she finds some options closed off. Her comments also illustrate how important it is for students to interact with faculty who can help them think through their ideas at that early stage. In Gabriella's case, she was lucky enough to find a faculty member who helped her focus on a topic that was really exciting for her:

I think it is an interesting lesson in how people might choose a topic. I was in a philosophy program, but I was inclined to be an empirical researcher, which is an odd duck in a philosophy program. And I was interested in, actually the topic I was interested in first was inclusion of women in research studies . . . So I went to a couple of people in the department of philosophy to propose this idea and ask them to be members of my dissertation committee, and they turned me down because they thought it was too sociological, not philosophical enough. So I was rather discouraged about that. And I went to—I met with a person who basically agreed in principle to be a part of my committee without a topic yet, and he made me sit down, and we went through this exercise where he said, "Okay, talk to me about the things you are interested in." And so I just started to talk. And he said, "Okay, tell me what you do at work." So I started to tell him what things, you know, I was doing at work. And you know, we talked for probably two hours. And at one point, he said to me, "That's it!" and I said, "What do you mean, that's it?" And he said, "That's your topic." I said, "Why?" He said, "You got so excited when you started to talk about it. So that's what you have to write about, that's what you have to do your dissertation on." And so that was really the first step in selecting a topic, and I think it was actually excellent advice because, as you know, the dissertation takes a lot of time and a lot of energy and a lot of focus, and there are some tedious aspects to doing it. You have to really be interested in what you're learning and writing. Otherwise, you can find it hard to finish.

Kate also described the somewhat serendipitous way in which she came to realize that the topic for her dissertation did not need to be her life work but was an opportunity to shape her future in research:

I understood the process and how tedious it could be, and one of the hardest problems I had was narrowing my question down so I could do it within my lifetime. And there was a good friend of mine, who told me about this woman who had just happened to talk a lot about research and how to do it and how to narrow down your subject matter, and she basically told me that I didn't have to do my whole research in one question, but this was one study that I needed to design and implement within a short period of time so that I could complete my dissertation. And then I could build my program of research on that afterwards, should I be so inclined or have the support to do so. And so it was through her guidance that I was then able to narrow down my subject matter. . . . And it's really interesting, there's a lot of times in my life where I was ready for a change or I needed some guidance, or I needed some insight, and somebody just kind of appears (laughs). It's funny how things just kind of fit together. . . . It not only provided the foundation for this dissertation, it also provided my link into the institute where I now work. So I guess what I would say is the dissertation process is not only the research process or the data that you get or what you publish, but it's also making connections with people and with opportunities that perhaps you would never, ever have thought of being qualified to do, or able to do, but because of the relationships you build with people along the way, it makes doors open that perhaps would not have been there before.

As students choose a topic and move on to the main phase of their dissertation project, the lack of clear and timely communication on important steps in the research process can cause frustration and add to the overall feeling of mystery. Celeste, who was completing her dissertation in a city several states away from her graduate school, encountered such problems. She felt she received ill-timed advice from her committee on what approach they wanted her to take toward certain details in her research:

It's like, "Well, this is looking good, but why don't you try this or that?" Well why didn't I know that before I wrote that chapter?

Celeste even felt the overall method she was expected or allowed to use for her research was not made clear to her early enough in the process:

I didn't have that information, and didn't get the feedback until I had submitted that. So I just about quit then. I was very frustrated. It was—probably my situation is a little unique in the fact that my committee members are all in Chicago, so I don't have anybody to go in and strangle over this. But it was very frustrating. And I asked because in preparation for the dissertation phase, we had to be very familiarized with not only quantitative and qualitative but historical and philosophical as well. And so, after being educated or not educated in whatever the process was, I felt like it just fell short on their end for not telling me that no, you can't do the philosophical or the historical. And that was just completely omitted from anything until the proposal was sent in.

Stella's advisor did not provide her with a framework for what the dissertation should be:

I felt like I was figuring out a lot of it as I went along. I don't think at any point really was there this discussion either on my own or with my advisor, like, oh, this is how you do it. . . . There wasn't any time at which I could have sat down and said, so *that* is a dissertation. And I figured it out.

Mary also found that the process and steps were not well communicated, which was particularly frustrating for her since she prides herself on organization and planning when she is managing projects in her own career:

> It was just so un-user friendly getting from step to step, and it was the most uncoordinated, I mean I am a very good project manager, and I put together a work plan, and there's no rigor around that part of doing a dissertation in academe. They're so loosey-goosey, and so, "Oh, I forgot to tell you! That form is due in a week; you're going to need these eight signatures on it, so . . ." "Oh, that might be a good idea; we should probably get everyone together and let them take a look at your proposal before you get started!" "Oops, did I forget to tell you, you can't submit to the IRB [Institutional Review Board] until you get through this class." There were all these rules that emerge spontaneously as you're going through the process. There was no one real good place to look to see what all the rules were. So that was very, very frustrating for me because I had a lot of time management rigor, and I had set up a timeline that I couldn't meet because of unexpected things that I didn't know. . . . There was no one place to go to look; you would go and ask somebody, and you'd get different answers from every person. It was, I was constantly surprised . . . surprised that new stuff was coming up all the time . . . it just felt like . . . and I'm not saying it's wrong that it falls on the student, but it is very, very uncoordinated and stressful.

One reason Mary found this lack of coordination stressful and frustrating was that she wanted to focus on the intellectual aspects of her dissertation process rather than the external steps:

> It wasn't an obstacle as much as it was . . . you have intellectual burdens during the process, and these were just logistical burdens that I felt like I needed my secretary to come with me (laughing) to handle all this stuff. And I handled it all myself . . . in fact, I did it all myself, but I felt, God, at one point, I would have easily paid to have somebody sending me reminders and doing some of that stuff because it was just a lot of little piddly things to keep track of and to follow up on. So, it wasn't that it was . . . I know it's an

expected, you have to do it, and I tried to do it with grace and positive attitude, but sometimes I would just go home and go, I can't believe this; it's just like insanity—the amount of things you have to do to get this thing in.

In contrast to the frustrations voiced by Mary and Celeste, Audrey suggested that no person could know how to do all the steps of the process until she was doing it, and that is just how it has to be—it is not necessarily anyone's fault, and it is not necessarily avoidable by better communication about steps and process:

> *Audrey:* I think that I knew the big picture, which is what they tell you: it has to be an original piece of research. And then the rest of it, the positional stuff and the quality, you know it has to be a certain quality, but you don't really know until you get into it, and you start having drafts come back to you, and you realize that—it was—that they had a standard, a particular . . . so it has to be a certain thing, but it has to be presented in a certain way as well. And I don't think I knew it would be like that until I was about half-way through the process (laughs). Because you know, people can tell you this all you like, but until you're actually doing it and seeing what passes and what doesn't, it's very difficult to know that.
> *Researcher:* So it wasn't so much that you felt like people could have or should have told you more, it's more that you felt like you had to find that out on your own anyway?
> *Audrey:* I think so, yeah.

Similarly, Eleanor found that advice—suggesting steps for her to take in her dissertation process—from her advisor or friends intending to be helpful could not help her because she needed to see the bigger picture. Seeing that bigger picture—how all the steps fit together—was something she had to do on her own:

> If I feel from them that, if I believe that their view is it's those steps alone that would get me to complete it, it doesn't—because

I guess I know in my heart and my mind that even if I follow a perfect formula, the steps will only be making sense if I am making the proper commitment, and if I am keeping the right goal in front of me. So I think one thing that bothers me is, I guess I realize only I can address these fears because they will always be present, and what I have to keep doing is putting them in context by focusing on what I care about and want to do and believe is right. And that involves continually . . . it's gotta be that I make a commitment to asserting the idea, and unless that commitment is made, all the right steps in the world won't get me there. So it's not necessarily that people's suggestions for steps hinder; because if I've made the proper commitment and I'm involved in the sort of process where I am focusing on the right things, the steps can be helpful. But even if someone tells me steps that *might* be helpful, they won't be because I'm just seeing all the branches and not seeing what it is that holds them up. I don't know how else to put it.

Most of the women talked about the difficulty of transitioning to a new and more complex form of writing for their dissertation. As Audrey's thoughts above suggest, part of the mystery of the dissertation process comes from the inescapable fact that a dissertation is a new level and scope of writing unlike any of the student's previous coursework. Greta explained:

The level of writing for your dissertation is . . . we're used to writing, well I found this, I found this and I found this. When you're writing your dissertation, the writing is: I found this. And this reveals this, this reveals this, this reveals this. It's almost like you have to write one page to put—to lay it all out. The next page—so how I'm ever going to think about this—and you have to write the synthesis. That no one ever tells you about.

Eleanor described this frightening leap from coursework to the dissertation quite dramatically, likening it to facing the jump off a cliff:

You don't want to get lost in discussing what's already been said, or anticipating how people will challenge it. After you consider all those things, to me, if it's a dissertation you also have—it almost feels like jumping off a cliff but sort of going back and getting to the heart of the matter—and you're going to have to leave aside a lot of things.

Audrey described the big leap caused by the increased complication in the kind of thinking, writing, and structure she had to employ for her dissertation as compared to her coursework:

> *Audrey:* And it took a long time, and I couldn't, for the first year or so, I couldn't get into any kind of groove. It was such a big leap, and sometimes, I didn't understand what he was saying—it seemed much more theoretical to me, and what I was doing was so much more complicated than anything I'd dealt with before—that working out how to present it was a real problem . . . and searching out how to do that and in what way that that makes sense. And also just the structure of a much longer work was, you know, difficult to get into, and again, I think that was something that I just had to learn as I went along. It wasn't a skill that was in the formal research papers that we'd done.
> *Researcher:* So even though you'd been trained pretty thoroughly, the leap was extreme?
> *Audrey:* Yeah, it was the distance I think between being in a class and having someone for all intents and purposes who was personally training me to do this.

Kim struggled specifically with the writing itself more than the research because she found herself trying to convey to her readers a large amount of complex material from her research in a way that would be clear and logical:

Yes, the hardest part of the entire process, because I love bench research, I love exploring ideas, but I felt like, that I wouldn't be able to communicate it all in, um, a logical, readable manner. So I read a lot about "let your writing be a story," "tell a story," and that was very helpful to me.

Kim also struggled with the writing process because of lack of confidence in her own writing ability even though she had successfully written many papers in her coursework:

No, I needed, that's another weakness of mine, I needed validation for some, from someone who I thought was a good writer. . . . I would write, rewrite and rewrite it, rewrite and rewrite it until finally I had, I felt it was in good enough shape that I was (laughs with some self-consciousness) I was willing to show it to somebody (laughing) . . . Oh 'cause I never, I absolutely don't have very much confidence in my writing ability. It has a long psychological history, and so I would write to the point where I thought I wouldn't be humiliated if you want to know the exact truth.

Martha helped herself overcome any intimidation from the new level of writing by breaking it down into skills and approaching it systematically:

Well, you know, I approached this as a job. And so I tried to tear it apart to say, "Okay, what are the different skills I'm gonna need?" um, externally, as well as, "What are the skills I need, um, for myself?" So I had somebody that would help me with text writing. I also had somebody that would help me, that was kind of a, a style and format sort of person, . . . who would like make sure my grammar was correct and that I wasn't too, and you know I wanted to find that balance between the technical writing and then the [disciplinary] aspect and then ensuring that, as it read, it flowed, and it was easy to read.

Gretchen worried about the quality of her writing not only because of the complexity but because of the style she believed she needed to adopt—a scholarly and elegant language:

Probably, what I worried about was that was the writing—was it good enough? Um, I worried that I wasn't as good a philosopher or an ethicist as all those people I was in class with because there was a big ethics component to my dissertation. And I worried that I wasn't going to be able to explain that in the same kind of scholarly, elegant way that those philosophers can write, um, or talk (laughs). I think that you have to develop that over a whole, long period of time. Um, but I did it.

The leap from coursework to dissertation writing also manifested in a new and different kind of support from classmates and feedback from mentors, as these women moved from energizing classrooms, where they received detailed and timely feedback from course instructors, to being out on their own, receiving very different (and sometimes significantly less) feedback from advisors. Mary found it difficult for someone with her personality type to move from the classroom to more independent research:

Support . . . um, it is a very lonely process. And I don't know if you know Myers-Briggs at all, but I'm an extrovert. I'm an E47; the scale only goes to 50, so I loved class. I loved being in class. I loved working in groups. I loved group assignments. I loved . . . I didn't mind writing on my own, but I really got a lot of energy out of being . . . I saw three cohorts go past me because it took me four years to finish the coursework, and I didn't mind 'cause every new group was another . . . just great people. And so when I finished the coursework, I feel that it was kind of a solitary journey for a year.

Celeste, who did her doctoral work long distance and thus, had not come to depend on the support or energizing effect of classmates, commented instead on the difficulty of shifting to a mode of less frequent and detailed help and feedback:

I had to figure it out as I went along. Honestly, I think there was more help during the coursework, and, in fact, one was on design—it was trying to help you unfold the process that you would be going through. But I think once I got into the dissertation area, I felt a bit more on my own. I really did. I don't think there was a lot of help as far as focusing—I know there wasn't. You get—after I finished that course and at the end of that course, I had a topic that was still too broad. It was too broad for me to do. But that was the end of it, but at least it was—these are the requirements, and this is the process, and some finish it quicker, and some take longer, and blah blah blah—all that I was told, but it was through a course, it was not through an advisor, it was not one-on-one. So once I started, I kind of felt thrown to the wolves a bit. I did. I felt like I was on my own with this.

Just as Celeste felt "thrown to the wolves" by the more self-directed process of writing a dissertation as opposed to coursework, Louise found that she wanted feedback at a very early stage, simply to make sure she was on the right track with her approach, structure, and style, but her advisor was unwilling to give her feedback of the kind she sought:

Well I just wanted to know if structurally that's what it was, and if you know, if I had made my case, that's what I wanted to know. All the clean-up and all that stuff, I just wanted to know, "Is this what a chapter is? Is that how you make an argument? You organize it that way?" That's all I wanted at that point.

Celeste encountered similar difficulties—wanting feedback early on and finding she got the feedback she needed too late in her writing process. She wanted to be able to have questions answered before putting her ideas into a piece of nearly-finished writing:

Well, the proposal that had to go through was the three chapters, your introduction, your bibliography, your methodology, and your literature. And the proposal kept getting returned, "Be more specific with so-and-so, is this really helping, is this what you're looking for, I wouldn't use this," but it was always after I'd done the work, and then I got the suggestions back. I didn't feel like I had the opportunity to ask questions in the process of writing the proposal.

Eventually, Louise came to realize the adjustments she had to make to the type and timing of feedback she could expect, but that did not necessarily change the kind of feedback she *wanted*:

I realized later, you can't send a draft to your professors. They take everything so seriously—even if I had said, "This is a draft, I just want to know I'm on the right path. Is this what it is, a 40-page chapter? You deal with this here, you deal with that there?" This is what I wanted.

Eleanor expressed strikingly similar thoughts when she was asked what ideal communication would be like between an advisor and a dissertation writer:

Ideally? As much communication as could be possible, and some means for the person writing the dissertation to send along different thoughts on what they have, not only about the topic but also about the process and their strategy and to have some sort of little junk box, that it was known that the advisor would look at that when it was convenient for them, and only respond in a way that was convenient for them, so that it could be quite low key, and yet the communication could be in place. So something that wouldn't be high-stakes communication.

Eleanor went on to explain that low-stakes communication would allow for informal language in an unpolished work, with a promise and understanding up front of no judgment on the lack of polish or the informality. She wished there could be:

. . . a casual way to get input, where there wouldn't be the feeling that the advisor had to necessarily take a tremendous amount of time to annotate every portion of what's submitted, but some kind of agreement, you know, I'm aware that there's tons of spelling errors and there's no citations yet and there are still three quarters of the chapter that has to be done, but could you read this and just write a brief paragraph or a couple of sentences, or leave a couple of messages on my answering machine to tell me if this is going down the right avenue or if I need to take a different approach.

One solution for a dissertation writer to find the kind of feedback she wants, at the stage she wants it, is to seek feedback from colleagues or peers or from someone who is qualified but is not a committee member. Naomi found great help from a colleague at her workplace:

Um, especially because I, I threw ideas past her, and I would, I would say, "Well, what do you think about this? What do you think about that?" Um, and she would give me *really* good feedback. And then, um, I'd send the papers past her as well. . . . And she gave me very targeted feedback on how to improve it. In fact, *much* better than anybody on my committee. Perhaps, it's because my topic was *so* specialized that no one on my committee knew anything about it? And so I really needed somebody who was in the field, who knew what they were talking about, had been through the dissertation process, and understood exactly what my committee was looking for.

The mystery these women tried to navigate came from a lack of communication from their committees and graduate programs, from the transition (or flying leap!) from coursework to dissertation writing, and from the adjustment to a new kind of independence expected of them that often resulted in feedback that was less detailed, helpful, or timely than the writer felt she needed. The women also struggled with confidence and skill in writing in the sophisticated voice required by a dissertation. Gretchen's words in talking about her struggles with writing capture what many of the women felt as they neared completion of their dissertations—a hesitant but proud acknowledgment, "Um, but I did it." Somehow, despite the mystery and the difficulty of the leap from coursework to dissertation writing, many of them reached the point where they could say, "Um, but I did it."

Stuck, Lost, and Confused

Many of the women we interviewed went through one or more periods of time where they found themselves stuck, lost, or confused in the overwhelming experience of the dissertation process. These periods of time tended to be stressful, and the women struggled to find their way out of them. One key to escaping these periods was to identify the causes of being stuck, lost, or confused. Some of the women reported that life itself tended to be a distraction that could cause stalls and periods of being stuck, but they also noted that going through a bad phase with their dissertation adversely affected the rest of their lives. One solution several women found was simply to step away, psychologically or physically, from their project for a day or two or longer.

Louise occasionally found herself feeling lost and confused and unable to make progress, which was very stressful to her. She was unsure whether the stress, in part, caused the feeling of being lost and confused, as she struggled to understand the material she was studying:

> I had maybe two moments during a year where it would be a month or it would be like two or three weeks I was really, I was really, really stressed, and I was worried because I couldn't make sense of the documents.

Gretchen had similar feelings that, for her, translated into something she identified as writer's block. This block was characterized by the same experience voiced by Louise—the feeling that she did not even understand what she was reading:

> Ah, I remember the process of analysis being very much like writer's block. . . . And so there would be times when I would just have this writer's block, where I'd be looking at the screen and it would be, "I don't know what this is telling me." And, um, what would help that would be going to the literature again and, um, just reading how people, reading the words of other researchers and how they were describing things . . . I could see how they were forming their words and thinking and labeling.

Eleanor stated that one reason she tended to get lost or stuck was because she had trouble seeing the connection between her research and writing process and the actual product she was trying to produce:

> It's not going to be sufficient that if you use a certain process, you'll end up with a certain product; it's not that relation, but if you want to end up with the sort of product where you have

produced something unique that engages the reader in a certain kind of thinking and challenges them and challenges you as well, and if you want to end up with a product that is attempting to assert an idea and not just be an exercise, it seems to me that to end up with that product requires that you go through this process. So the process is linked with the product, but it's not sufficient necessarily to produce it either.

Eleanor found also that she had trouble seeing the big picture of how all her research and ideas fit together into a whole because, sometimes, it just seemed too complex:

Sometimes, I've become very frightened as I start doing the research and realizing all the different avenues, and realize okay now I need to take and make a commitment to one part of this idea, I need to discuss the idea without necessarily referring to other things so that I can start restating and re-expressing what I believe is truly important. I've become scared sometimes at the enormous amount of different little avenues I could go down and the fear if I return to this main part of the idea where there's not a lot of literature on it, will it really work . . . ? There's tons of details that need to be taken care of, and each one requires additional steps.

In addition to the periods of confusion and feeling stuck because of the overwhelming nature of the research project itself that others experienced, Gretchen found herself occasionally slowing down or getting stuck because she would become distracted—sometimes necessarily—by other elements of her life. When we asked her what sorts of things had distracted her, she replied:

I don't know: little things. Was the car going to break down? Was I gonna make it to Pittsburgh for an appointment that was important? I'd worry about the car, I'd worry about paying for gas.

Several other women found they would have to take weeks or even months off from their dissertation work to attend to needs such as sick family members, teenage children going through a rough time, or problems at their own workplace. (Some of these stories are detailed in Chapters 3 and 4.)

In contrast, Eleanor tended to find that things happened the other way around for her. When she found herself stuck on her dissertation, she would start to feel like she was stuck in other aspects of her life as well:

The biggest thing I've discovered that can get me stuck is that it's easy to take that process and look at all of that and think, oh, well now, there are compound instances, where I'm digging a deeper and deeper hole for myself, and now I have all these additional holes I have to get myself out of (laughs)! And so, in a way, it's almost like when I start going through the process in a way that is not focusing on the right things, it almost ends up feeling like a virus that's replicating itself into other areas of my life, and so the stuck part ends up not only being not only stuck in the hole I'm trying to get out of with the dissertation, but trying to get out of the hole I'm in, in the way I'm living in my life, and the perception that I haven't met these other goals. So the way to try to get beyond that is to . . . not be looking at the spillover itself as having power. And not thinking that, okay if I'm stuck on the dissertation, it's actually going to invade all other areas of my life and I'm powerless to get beyond it.

Eleanor found herself, at times, in a vicious cycle where her frustrations and lack of progress with her dissertation made her want to spend even more time on research and writing, which caused her to feel like she was neglecting other important aspects of her life. In turn, that "spillover" made her feel more out of control and less able to re-establish confidence and command over her own research process.

Because we heard from many of the women we interviewed that they became stuck or experienced writer's block at times, we asked them what they did to overcome these troubling periods in their work. Naomi dealt with this problem often enough that she had an established routine to help her move past it. She knew she was particularly prone to get stuck after receiving feedback from her advisor:

> I did a lot of venting to my husband. I went on a *lot* of long runs. Usually what I would do, I would get back a lot of comments from my advisor, and I would just see red. And, you know, I was just *furious* and *irritated*, and just feeling like I wanted to harm someone. Um, obviously I never would, but I, I was just, I mean I would be *so upset* about it, and so I would go running or go away from it for a while, give myself usually, I don't know a couple hours, sometimes 24 hours, but usually not that much, because I like to just get things done, so like ripping off a Band-Aid, you gotta do it quickly.

Kate had a similar approach to overcoming the times when she felt lost or stuck. Like Naomi, she would find ways to step away and let herself clear her thinking and her mood:

> Sometimes, you have to remove yourself from your general stress level and work level and things that are going on in order to write.... I love the beach. And so when I would get too tied up or couldn't think straight anymore 'cause I was so tired of looking at the data, I would go walk on the beach in my winter coat and just think. So you need some time to think and process what you're trying to review, and read, and put together in a story. Um, the other thing about the beach is I love water, and it kind of renews me, and so I could go out and look at the ocean in between things and get some energy back. I also just had my computer in my room and didn't have anything else I had to do, no places I had to be, there wasn't much open down at [the beach] in the winter, so I didn't have any distractions.

Both Naomi and Kate learned to recognize what triggered their less productive times and when they needed to step away to change gears and clear their minds. Venting to loved ones, exercising, and getting away to a new locale seemed to help them the most. For each person writing a dissertation, it is important to learn to recognize and accept these unproductive times for what they are, and know how best to step away, recharge, and refocus.

Isolation

The challenge of navigating through the mysteries of the dissertation process and of making it through periods of confusion and frustration can be made harder by feelings of isolation. The dissertation process requires a lot of time alone in intense concentration and focus, and that, in itself, can be isolating. In addition, many dissertation writers are likely to find that many of the important people in their lives—family and colleagues—have little experience with or understanding of what is involved in writing a dissertation. Thus, while focusing on work that is very important to them, they are unable to share details about the process or their frustrations or joys in a way that the people who form their usual support systems can fully understand. And perhaps the greatest isolation comes from the overwhelmingly intense and large nature of the task, which can consume a dissertation writer to the point where she feels she cannot give enough of herself to those around her.

Most of the women we interviewed found that they had to spend all or most of their dissertation time working alone. Otherwise, they could not be productive or they got distracted or more stressed. Mary, who is very social and normally prefers to work collaboratively with others, tried to coordinate her work with a dissertation work group, but she found it did not help her, or possibly made things worse:

> The one time I met with a [dissertation work] group, they made me more anxious. I just thought, if I'm going to meet with a group twice a month for three hours, I could write part of a chapter in three hours or update my literature search. So, I just kind of pulled away from that, and it was just isolating 'cause what I'd end up doing is taking days off of work to be able to go to work alone somewhere to write.

Greta found that the constant need for seclusion so that she could accomplish her goals adversely affected her mood, leaving her feeling lonely and depressed:

By the time you get to your dissertation, you're working all alone. All through doctoral coursework you're with other people, but when you're down to the dissertation, it's you and me and the front of a piece of paper. It's really lonely. The only—the most depressed I have ever gotten in my life was when I was writing my dissertation. I'm a very positive, happy person, but I was in the throes of despair. If I would have been weak and taken medication I would have said—you know this is the time—I remember reading, um, Norman Vincent Peale, I think *In God We Trust*. I read that book every day. And I tried everything—everything that they tell you to do to lift yourself up, I tried to do all of it 'cause it was hard, I mean that writing . . . and . . . it's lonely. It's lonely work. And it's work that you gotta do.

Both Mary and Greta tended to be more social in their other work and in their daily lives, and the time alone necessitated by the dissertation process seemed to take more of a toll on them than on some women who normally prefer to work alone. But even some of the women who did not mind working alone *per se* found that the lack of understanding from colleagues or the lack of a consistent peer group caused them to feel isolated. Martha found herself among colleagues without comparable degrees who did not understand what she was going through:

When you're working in an environment where nobody else has a doctoral degree, and it's kind of like you know nobody understands what you're going through, nobody really gives that much of a crap about it. You know, it's sometimes kind of a lonely journey because you're the only one that can do it, you're the only one that's involved in it.

Celeste found that even her peers in her graduate program could not serve as a source of significant support for her, since they had their own concerns to be thinking about and since that peer group kept changing:

> They all have their own lives, and they all have their own problems, probably similar to mine. Also, people that you start out with in the program are not necessarily the people that you end up with. Because they have—some of the courses they don't—they won't do well and they can't move on, they have to repeat—the comps kicked a lot of fannies. And in fact, you have to get it and if you don't, you're out, and a lot of people fail out during the comps stage. So it's like—a different crowd than I started with. So I haven't had a lot of collegial support.

Perhaps most surprisingly, many of the women we interviewed found that the dissertation made them feel isolated in ways outside their research and writing process. Because the dissertation is so all-consuming, some of these women found it difficult to turn off that part of their lives to relax or just be themselves. When we asked Audrey why she sometimes felt isolated, she replied:

> Partly it was, there was no good down time. I didn't have anyone who was around. I was living on my own at the time, for the majority of it. I didn't really have a space where I could say, okay, I'm done for the day, I'm going to stop this, and I'm going to go talk to somebody else. And that was when I felt isolated. It was when I wasn't doing the dissertation more than when I was concentrating on it. But after a while, it began to consume everything, and if I wasn't working on it, I felt bad for not working on it, so . . . if I went out and did anything else, I was twitchy and I would feel guilty, and even if I'd done ten hours that day on it, I would go out—if I did something else, if I watched TV, I felt guilty about it.

Thus, Audrey found that even when she tried to relax and seek out social interaction, she could not quite engage herself in it in the way she wanted.

Louise also found that the dissertation took enough of her that it threatened to close her off from the rest of her life:

It felt like, I'll be in the dissertation forever. This is how I felt, like I was in jail for the next 30 years. I mean, I knew it wasn't true, but it felt that way.

Callie talked about the dissertation's large influence on her life in a way that personified it; in her choice of language, she attributes to the dissertation its own needs and desires:

I think we forget that it's really such an important piece of work. It needs so much of you. It needs all of you emotionally and intellectually. It can't be a distant piece of work that you can put down and pick up; well, to me it can't.

As expressed by Callie and others, it seems that the dissertation process is almost unavoidably isolating. The research and writing require much time alone; colleagues and family members are likely not to understand all that is involved and the stresses that are caused by the process, and the dissertation can be so all-consuming that even relaxation time can feel artificial, strained, or compromised. This feeling of isolation is likely to be one of the most difficult aspects of the dissertation experience for many people and can compound other troubling feelings like being lost and confused.

Positive Outcomes of the Mystery, Confusion, and Isolation

While we did hear reports of mystery, confusion, and isolation from nearly all of the women we interviewed, we were also struck by two women's observations that these aspects of the dissertation experience do not necessarily have to be entirely negative. Gretchen and Kim both spoke of positive outcomes from the mystery and confusion, finding that these aspects of their experience helped them to learn and to grow as researchers and individuals. Gretchen was intrigued by the sudden shift from structured courses to near-total self-direction and freedom:

When I got to the dissertation phase, after all the course work, the other piece that was interesting for me was, um, there was no syllabus for this. So I remember saying to one of the members of my committee, "Okay, so you want me to do this, and this, and when is that?" and, you know, asking for due dates and things like that. And I got this email that said well, this is solo work, this is, now you're on your own. We're here to consult with, but you need to be self-directed and move on. And that's all I needed to hear because it sort of set me up correctly for that next phase.

Once Gretchen confirmed and established that she was on her own, she pushed past her initial concerns and welcomed the challenge:

Oh, I thought, I felt alone when I heard, when I got that email, [that this is solo work]. And yet it confirmed what I really knew (laughs). That yeah, okay, this is the big one. You have to go, you can't be spoon-fed for this one. You have to really show that you can do what they've prepared you to do. And, um, so I think in that way it's a good lesson.

Kim appreciated the independence required and welcomed by her program, which allowed her to be the most important part of her own education:

I think one of the strengths of my program was that you were, you were always in the equation, you were not merely following directions. You had to use your own, um, creativity, your own strength of character . . . You had resources in which you could go and ask for advice or ask for even sometimes help, like, "Help me!" you know . . . But as far—it was never following directions.

In addition to the independence required of her in her program, Kim also specifically appreciated that the individual steps necessary to complete her dissertation were not dictated to her or even spelled out at all:

I think that's the strength of the doctoral preparation, that you learn how to do research, but you also learn what it means to have an idea and a problem, and how to solve that problem, or how to find an answer to a scientific question or an idea or what have you. . . . Sometimes, I think as a doctoral candidate that you wish somebody would say, "Do A and do B, and you will get your little degree." But in the end, I don't think that serves you well.

Going even further in exploring her beliefs on this issue, Kim realized that she was actually excited by the mystery of it, by having to find her own way:

Yes, because I think that from what I've learned from science, that there's never one formula. And that is the excitement of discovery, where you can discover a different way, or tweak a standard procedure, so that you get slightly better results. So I think that is true in the dissertation . . . I think that is one of the lessons you learn in the dissertation process.

Reflections on the Stories

This feeling lost, this perceived lack of support and guidance, and running into problems and not knowing who can help, may be the most difficult aspect of the dissertation process to overcome. Celeste expressed this point most dramatically:

You reach this point, and I remember, my [department] chair [at my workplace] told me, "You know, I can't tell you how many people get to this point and then they quit. And they're always ABD." And he said, "Because you're going to find out that there are lots of problems."

It is our hope that hearing these stories of confusion and isolation can, paradoxically, give encouragement to women experiencing the same feelings during their dissertation process. Kim's attitude may provide helpful guidance—"There's never one formula. And that is the excitement of discovery"—but not all students writing a dissertation may be able to find excitement in the mystery that allows for discovery.

Heidegger's philosophy may offer some help here. He discusses a concept he calls "openness to the mystery," an attitude he sees human beings struggling with.[1] As we aggressively expand our science and technology in order to understand our world, to dominate it by solving every puzzle and shining light on every unknown, Heidegger says we forget to leave time for reflection and for the wonder that openness to the mystery can give us. Instead, we humans have grown more accustomed to, and comfortable with, a type of thinking Heidegger calls calculative thinking:

> Whenever we plan, research, and organize, we always reckon with conditions that are given.... Thus we can count on definite results. This calculation is the mark of all thinking that plans and investigates ... calculative thinking computes. It computes ever new, ever more promising and, at the same time, more economical possibilities.... Calculative thinking never stops, never collects itself.[2]

Notice here that Heidegger says we are accustomed to having conditions given so that we can plan on definite results. We are used to being able to plan, to calculate, and when we cannot do so, we feel out of our depth. No wonder the women speaking in this chapter feel lost and overwhelmed when they find themselves in new, unexplored territory where very little is given, and definite results are difficult to count on or predict.

In contrast to this calculative thinking we humans are used to relying on, Heidegger calls us to engage in meditative thinking, which will help us remain open to the mystery. Meditative thinking can be much more difficult for us, as Heidegger explains: "It requires a greater effort. It demands more practice. It is in need of even more delicate care than any other genuine craft. But it must also be able to bide its time, to await as does the farmer, whether the seed will come up and ripen."[3] Meditative thinking asks us to leap into the unknown, to give ourselves time to ponder, to be less efficient and more reflective in our thinking process. In contrast to calculative thinking that never stops to collect itself, meditative thinking requires us to be patient, to go over the same paths again and again. Meditative thinking asks us to renounce willing, give up on everything being planned, and wait for the thoughts and revelations that may come to us, leaving open the possibility of what we are waiting for.[4] It asks us to "engage ourselves with what at first sight does not go together at all,"[5] so that we might find meaningful and surprising connections.

The women whose voices we hear in this chapter have very practical goals—to write a dissertation in order to get a doctoral degree, thus advancing their career and life opportunities. Within this practical context, it may seem difficult or even paradoxical to let go, to be open to the mystery, to welcome surprising connections. And yet, at least some of the dissertation process might require the writer to do just that. Some of it cannot be signaled ahead of time by advisors, cannot be planned by even the most dedicated, forward-thinking writer. As Kim said, "It was never following directions."

The good news is that, at least according to Heidegger, anyone can engage in meditative thinking and thus remain open to the mystery—it is something that humans are born able to do; it is part of our special nature.[6] And in thinking this way, we do not have to become lost or stumble around blindly. Our inquiry itself can serve as an "inconspicuous guide."[7] As a writer explores the possible paths for her dissertation, she may find the research itself guides her in a certain direction. The dissertation might be better, and the process less frustrating, if the writer lets the inquiry nudge her, rather than if she sticks to some initial, rigid plan.

Perhaps most practical in Heidegger's advice about meditative thinking is that we should start with what is closest to us.[8] For a student writing a dissertation, this might first mean choosing a topic she is engaged with and excited by, as Gabriella was encouraged to do by the faculty member who said to her, "That's it! . . . You got so excited when you started to talk about it. So that's what you have to write about, that's what you have to do your dissertation on." Starting with what is closest to a dissertation writer can also mean figuring out what skills and knowledge she already has that can help her, starting as much as possible with the things she knows how to do rather than getting overwhelmed by the mysterious big picture and the many things she fears she does not know how to do. If a writer thus starts on paths that are closest to her, she will likely find that those paths then connect to other paths that may now be clearer or seem a bit easier.

Readers who find themselves facing mystery, confusion, or isolation may want to ask themselves: What are the best steps toward choosing a topic and method? If these steps are not well communicated, can I suggest improvements in this communication for the sake of myself and others in my program? How can I make this scary leap from coursework to dissertation seem smaller? Can I break it into smaller, more familiar parts? What helps me get unstuck—venting, exercise, or a change of location? Are there ways I can help myself feel less isolated in general or for certain times in the day or week? Through addressing questions like these, the writer may find what Eleanor sought on her own journey—the ability to see not only all the branches but also what it is that holds them up.

Chapter 3

Realigning Relationships

My sister would come in every couple of hours, and she'd open the door to the suite, and she'd go, "Are ya done yet?" (laughing) And she asked me like 50 times in the four days! "Are ya done yet . . . you've been workin' on that awful long!" And you know the whole hotel room had books everywhere and stacks of paper everywhere and my computer and printed out pages of everything, but she'd ask, every few hours, "Are ya done yet?" So, if you read my acknowledgement page in the actual dissertation book, at the bottom, it says thank you to my sister, who really did support me a lot, and now I can finally say, "Yes, I am done."

— Mary

The women in our study talked about the impact their family and social relationships had on the process of writing their dissertations as well as the impact that the writing of the dissertation had on their relationships. In the long process of writing the dissertation, the women found that, many times, their relationships realigned as they themselves changed. This was expressed poignantly by Callie in her worry that her relationships with her partner and friends were affected by how she was changing through the process of writing her dissertation.

I thought, is it me changing? And I just—all my relationships are realigning.... There are conversations that I can't have anymore because I want to have ones that are more meaningful, because that's where I'm at.... So it does worry me, it does worry me. I don't really know if there's an answer to that in the long run. But right now I'm in this process.

The Stories

The women in this study juggled amazing responsibilities and struggled to find a balance in their lives between their work toward their degree and their relationships with family and friends. For some, the all-encompassing process of dissertating distanced them from relationships that they traditionally had found to bring comfort and stability in their lives. For others, the intensity of the dissertation process brought them closer to some of their family and friends. Women talked about how dissertating affected their relationship with life partners and other family members, friends, and co-workers and how these relationships affected the dissertation process. As illustrated by Mary's quote above, a sense of humor helped immensely to build and maintain strong and supportive relationships amidst the constant stress of the dissertation.

Life Partners

The women talked about how their life partners integrated themselves into the dissertation process. Struggling with not being able to care for the house and the children in their usual efficient way, the women were grateful when their partners accepted a less-than-organized household and helped out with chores. It was clear that most of the partners wanted very much to be supportive but did not really understand the dissertation process and why it would take so long and require such intensity. Almost all of the women noted that their partners worried about them not finishing the dissertation and wanted them to be done. As women told their stories, it was easy to picture the disrupted household with partners stepping in to help, or not, but at the same time, hoping against hope that the process would end soon.

Gretchen talked about how she had a conversation with her husband before she started school to decide whether to undertake doctoral studies, which they both knew would be an incredible stress for the whole family, and how he helped her to know that it was the right time to begin:

> I had just finished my master's, and I was on a roll, and he said, "Do you really want to do this? Because if you do, you need to do it now because we're going to have everybody in school at the same time down the road, and we can't have *three* of you in school at the same time!"

She explained that years later, after she was deep in the dissertation process, her husband helped her focus each day on getting something done with the dissertation:

> My husband would send me to my office after supper. He was afraid that I was not gonna get done. He was afraid I was gonna lose my momentum. And so he would just say, you know, "I'll do the dishes." He cooked, he did the dishes, he took care of the children, and he said, "You go do that" every night. And so I would go down into my little cave, which was my basement office. And I would either be transcribing or I'd be analyzing, reading, analyzing, re-reading . . . all that you do with qualitative research.

Greta also talked about how her husband worried that she would not finish. She wanted to be careful not to "contaminate" the home with her negative energy:

> My husband was at home saying, "Get done." Some people suggested to me that maybe this summer when my son was very sick, that maybe I should just slow down. And [my husband] would say, "No. Just get done, Greta. Just get done." So I had

a very strong message of: "Just get done." He didn't want me to contaminate my home any longer than it needed to be. It's hard when mothers go back to school, you know—they're not as happy. They don't do their work—someone's gotta pick up the slack. And he just wanted it done. He didn't want it hanging around the house for years and years and years. 'Cause I'd say, "Honey, some people take six to ten years," and he's just like "I don't want that around that long. Just get it over with." . . . He just, he knew how fun life is when it's done. So he just wanted it to be done. . . . He wanted me to have a workload that wasn't gonna kill me—not kill me but also contaminate the family by having mommy be so bitchy.

Martha described how she shared the household chores with her husband to get the support she needed:

I just let my husband know, you're probably not gonna hear from me for about 18 months. I'm gonna be here, but not really here. I'm gonna be working on this. And you know it was like, "Okay, just can you make the kids dinner? Make sure my clothes are clean?" "Sure, I can do that."

Louise talked about the emotional support she got from her husband and that it meant very much that he believed in her ability to complete the dissertation even though she had serious doubts:

My husband was wonderful. He would send me cards and tell me all the time that 90 per cent of the doing is just believing, and he was like, "Come on, you can do it, you can do it, there's so many people who did it, and you're smarter than they are. You can do it. It's nothing. It just has to be done." And he never, ever doubted that I could write a dissertation. Never. That still amazes me! And also that he would do all the stuff in the house. There were times I couldn't cook, and I said, "This week I have something due. You're on your own, and cook for me, please." And he would be like, "Okay." I mean I had to ask him because sometimes he would forget, and I would get angry, like, "You need to do this." But otherwise it worked out well. . . . I was not by myself. There was a stability in my life. . . . When I get down, I can talk to my husband, and I get a five-hour pep talk because I'm really down. I mean, when you live by yourself, you can't call somebody for four hours and cry all the time. I didn't have that very often, but I knew that he was there.

Claire also emphasized the emotional support she came to rely on from her husband:

Sometimes I would get so discouraged and it was hard to continue. Usually, I was working intensely and tuning everything out for hours at a time, but sometimes it would all come crashing down, and I'd just feel shell-shocked. I remember a time I'd gotten very discouraging and really, I thought, kind of mean feedback from my advisor, and I felt so defeated. My husband took me out for ice cream, and we just sat there, and he said, "Look, your advisor's being a jerk. Maybe he can't help it, but he's a jerk, and maybe you don't have to listen to him more than you absolutely have to." I remember just hearing that validation, that it wasn't me, it was that my advisor was being really insensitive, and really, I was doing fine—I really needed that to get back on track.

Callie felt supported by her partner but also struggled with how her relationship with him became more and more complex and frustrating because of her work on the dissertation. She felt like neither of them quite knew what to do. She talked about a situation where one of the members of her committee seemed to be making unreasonable demands, and she was extremely stressed. Her partner, Joe, wanted to be supportive but also intensely wanted her dissertation to be over. She struggled with wanting to talk to him about her stress but also realizing that he could not really understand what she was dealing with:

It was hard. And I got an email [from my committee member] the next day saying, "We're worried about you." Which made it even *worse*. I thought, oh my God, now they think I can't cope, and oh, oh, oh! So it was a really tough time, actually, it was really a crux for me, on lots of levels. You know, kind of personally, with my relationship with Joe, who is then saying to me, "I'm sick of you doing this PhD." Because I was totally obsessed. . . . I think talking about it, actually, in retrospect, helped me. Actually vocalizing it, because it got me to talk about it with Joe, and able to talk with him about how I felt, because this time, really, . . . I was just kind of hysterical with it all, . . . he was finding it very difficult that all I wanted to do, you know, in any of my free time, was to spend time with my work. But I think also you start communicating on a different level, you know. And I want to talk about things, on a certain level—because I feel kind of alienated from my friends . . . And what I *do* do is I arrange to see people. I arrange—one night a week is mine. So it'll come to that day, and I'll go out with friends, but I wasn't doing that with Joe.

As Callie dialogued with the researcher, she seemed to surprise herself with some of her insights that came through the reflective process:

> *Researcher:* So with your friends, even if it was sparse, you were setting aside time to maintain those relationships, at least at a bare minimum.
> *Callie:* Yes. Absolutely. But not with him.
> *Researcher:* Were you aware that you were doing that, or . . . ?
> *Callie:* I think I probably was. I think he just had to accept that. He had to accept that's what I was doing, you know, and I think—I do a lot with the kids, that was kind of, you know, don't be telling me, because I do a lot for this family, so it was kind of getting to the point where I was feeling kind of devalued. But that was it, the family as well, because I was doing so much family work, and then I was getting this criticism for being obsessed with the work, it was like, "What do you want me to do?"
> *Researcher:* And I do not want to read into what you are saying, so tell me if this is accurate, but it almost sounds like you felt—I don't know if it was an obligation, or a desire—to work to maintain the friendships, but then you didn't feel like you should have to do that, at least not in the same way, with your relationship with your partner?
> *Callie:* Yeah, that sounds a bit harsh I suppose, hearing it, but that's true. You know, he's really good, he's a lovely guy, he's a lovely man, but he wouldn't even want to aspire—he wouldn't want to talk about anything

academic. You know, if I talk about anything in terms of the philosophy I was trying to use, he'd make a joke. I could talk to him about the trauma aspect—he's very good on kind of an emotional level—and how that's made me feel. He might not understand, but he'd listen. But yeah, I don't know—the kind of benignness of it, and that sounds really awful. The kind of benignness of what we'd talk about, it was really starting to get to me, the frustration of it.

Researcher: And that's not something that was a problem before.

Callie: No. Absolutely it wasn't bothering me before. Because I was hearing probably benign at work, you know, banal, kind of everyday crap, that people talk about. But when you're doing a PhD on your own, you're kind of subsumed with this very complex material and reaching constantly, you want to talk about it, and also to have stimulation.

Callie's struggle with her emotions is poignant as she tries to reconcile her own emotional needs with being fair to Joe:

It isn't fair because I'm expecting him to be something that he isn't, I suppose, and expecting him to have a level of awareness and understanding. Because it would make me feel better. But my relationships with friends are kind of very removed, and when I see them, I don't have those kinds of conversations, if this is making any sense—when I see the girls and we go out, we'll have tea, we'll have a drink, and we'll catch up on our lives, and that's what I want. That's a release. But then Joe is the person I spend most of my time with, and I want to be able to share things. I've read all day, and I've been on my own all day, so he comes in from work, and I want to talk to him. "You know I've just . . .," and I was getting back humor. To which I wanted to say, "It's not funny, you know? It's really hard to understand this." And I think recognition of what I was doing, and again it was a matter of being able to turn to *him*, really. We did go out—we went away for a weekend—after this period. And we just talked about things and talked about how I felt about it and how he felt about it. You know, kind of this really, you need to bear with this process because it's really important.

And he knows it's really important to me, and I think about him understanding what it takes as well. Because his frustration about me being obsessed with it—since that point he's never mentioned that again. I think he's always known what it means to me, and he is very proud of me. So I think it's probably a realignment of relationships, you know, which has needed to be, to do this PhD.

Bubbles was the only participant who stated that she went through a divorce during her dissertation. She described how she believes the long hours of working on her research affected her relationship with her husband:

I got divorced during my PhD, so that was a time that understandably was rough. . . . Part of the reason why it didn't work was the realization that you have to work very long hours—or I did at the time. When you're doing research on animals, they don't wait to do things, you know you have to do it every day. When you're in the middle of an experiment, there's no way to like, push the pause button; no matter what is going on in your life, you have to deal with it. . . . And there was a lot of tension over money because we didn't have any, and who was going to do all the chores because it wasn't going to be me because I worked so many long hours, and we were both commuting at that time. So this pile of resentment built up in me because I was working 60 to 70 hours a week, and he was basically not doing that, not working. He was going to school also for an undergraduate degree, so he was a returning student, after being in the military. So he just played golf and enjoyed his life, and then I would get home, and he would say, "What's for dinner tonight?" And this is the life I was living. So my—I really just turned into someone that I did not like because this resentment built up and I was very angry. And I started doing all this research on gender roles and why we have to . . . they sell us this thing, like, you can have it all, but you really can't unless you have someone who is supportive, which he was not. And so it just fell apart, pretty quickly.

As Bubbles continued, she described an interesting insight that came out of the broken relationship, in that the tedious nature of the current stage of her research project was actually a comfort to her in her state of confusion and helped her keep order in her life:

> That was an unhappy experience, but in some ways, looking back on it, I do think that I used work as a refuge. . . . I mean I would put these labels on these boxes, and they would all have to be lined up just perfectly straight, and I would look at it and think, that's right. This is all working. This is all perfect. And this is how I wanted it, and now it's like this. And somehow, that was very comforting to me at the time. So the thing that nobody tells you about doing scientific research when you're just thinking about all these good ideas is how tedious and boring and ridiculous a lot of the stuff is that you have to do. I had to count 10,000 eggs every day—tiny little insect eggs—it's just horrible. And I don't really enjoy doing that kind of stuff. I mean it's something you have to do, but, in that period of my life, I don't know that I enjoyed it, but it was comforting. It was something you could do without thinking a lot, and my brain was too disordered to think because I was going through all this. So it ended up kind of being fine even though it was a very traumatic experience, but the place that I was in my research, I could just focus on those kind of menial, tedious, monotonous tests and actually get a lot of work done but not have to—that was a time when I couldn't have done a lot of writing or anything like that. That would not have been—so that was another fortuitous thing, that it worked out that I was doing things that I could still do. And in fact it even brought me a lot of comfort and peace of mind at that time. There's just a place that when I put things like this, and I come back, they're still like that, they're still in the same place.

The stories from the women about relationships with their partners during the dissertation process were both inspiring and poignant. Since all of the partners of the women we interviewed were men, the differing traditional roles of male and female became clear, as the men struggled to try to be helpful with traditionally female roles in the family but found it difficult to conceal the frustration that was right below the surface. The length of the dissertation process was a constant stress on the relationship. The women were intent on writing a quality dissertation, but their partners often did not understand what this was. And this lack of understanding should not be surprising, since even the women did not really understand it. Even those women who talked about very supportive partners and how the stress brought them closer acknowledged the difficulties of maintaining stable relationships amidst the process of writing a dissertation.

Family Support

As noted in Chapter 2, most women found the dissertation an isolating experience and talked at length about how much they needed support from family. Mary, who balanced a high-pressure job with caring for a family with teenagers while also doing her dissertation, approached her family relationships with a similar type of take-charge approach as she used in her career. She stated that she did not have a lot of family support, but colored this with good-natured humor as she described how she managed to build the support that she needed. In the end, she knew her family and friends were proud of what she accomplished. Talking about her mother, she laughed as she said:

My mom was sweet and clueless. You know, "Good luck," every week, "I hope you're doing okay."

She was more specific about the rest of her family:

My family wasn't particularly supportive; they were sick of it. They'd had it. They pretended to be supportive (laughing), but then they're like, "What's for dinner?" Like you're in a zone of writing, writing, writing, writing, writing, writing . . . 6:30, quarter of seven, 7:10 . . . and they're like "Mommy, Mommy, what's for dinner?" You're like, "God, nothing!" I don't care if I ever eat again, . . . I'm gonna really crank out this Chapter 5 or whatever. So what does support look like for them? My husband didn't leave me, but nobody really . . . no one in my family like picked up the yoke and carried it through. Nobody was like, "Don't worry; we'll go grocery shopping for the next six months. Don't worry, Mom, I'll put together"... I mean I have a 19-, 15-, and 11-year old. They could have done a lot more, but they just, they had no ... I don't think they were dialed in enough to what I was doing and what it meant. It wasn't until the actual manuscript was completed, and I had some of the drafts bound at Kinko's, and my 19-year-old daughter looked at it, and it was like, "Oh my God, this is like a book." When she actually saw what I had finished, saw the data, and it was quantitative, a lot of data sets and graphs, and she was like "How did you do this? I can't believe you did this . . . how do you know how to do regression analysis?" She's in calculus . . . "How do you know how to do regression analysis . . . you're a nurse!" You know, so at the end, they had more of an awareness of it, but in the process of it, they were just like, I don't know, they were fine, but I wouldn't say, "Oh God, without my family I couldn't have done it." There were plenty of days when I wished they had just left, (laughing) 'cause without my family, I *could* have done it . . . a lot easier!

In spite of her dramatic descriptions of the lack of family support, Mary found a way to make her family relationships work for her:

I thought, how can I make this writing experience more fun. So I took my daughter and my sister to California for five days, got a beautiful place on the water, and basically I said to them, "You guys have to entertain each other, and I'm gonna write all day, but we're going out some place really nice for dinner, and I'm going to get up early, and I'm going to work 'til five or six o'clock, and then you pick the restaurant, and we'll go out to dinner. So we went out four nights to these wonderful seafood places. My daughter went boy-watching with my sister (laughs), and then they did something every day. They went on the water, they did just fun things. I'd have to say, in four days, I did probably 40 hours of writing and really got the thing in beautiful shape. So what was supportive was having them there; they were busy doing their own stuff, but having them there for dinner . . ., and my sister would come in every couple of hours, they'd come back, and she'd open the door to the suite, and she'd go, "Are ya done yet?" (laughs) And she asked me like 50 times in the four days! "Are ya done yet . . . you've been workin' on that awful long!" And you know the whole hotel room had books everywhere and stacks of paper everywhere and my computer and printed out pages of everything, but she'd ask every few hours, "Are ya done yet?" So if you read my acknowledgement page in the actual dissertation book, at the bottom, it says thank you to my sister, who really did support me a lot, and now I can finally say, "Yes, I am done." (laughs) So that, in particular, was very supportive to me.

Stella felt that it was important to tell her story about her mother. Her story provides a hint of the complexity that a dissertation brings into family relationships:

I'd like to relate one story. And I'll preface it by saying, I love my mom, my mom is really wonderful, and she's very supportive, and when she said this to me, she meant it in a very supportive way. But at one point, this was when I was preparing for the oral exams before my dissertation, I was talking to my mom about how stressed out I was, and this is just so overwhelming, and she told me, "Well, how you do on those tests isn't important to me. I just want you to have babies. I just want to have grandbabies." (laughs) It was meant as, "I love you no matter what," and my mom was also kind of going through a little bit of an "I want grandkids" period, so it was the kind of thing that was coming up quite a bit. I finally had to call her on it and explain to her, well I was actually kind of blunt about it, but it got the point across. But she, that was something that is very important to her . . . It wasn't something she was trying to impose on me, but, nonetheless, not what I needed to hear. And I told her that, "Mom, that's not what I need to hear." But yeah, I think that was her way of saying, "I love you no matter what."

Some women forged new relationships with their parents as the long dissertation process immersed them in unexpected life events that surprisingly led to new and satisfying ways of relating. Monique found that after the death of her father, she became closer to her mother:

My dad died during the time of the dissertation, my daughter had to have major surgery, my mom had a stroke and came to live with me. I was frustrated that all those kinds of things happened, and I could've easily just said I have to stop. I have to focus on this now. But I knew if I did that, it would be that much harder for me to get back in the swing and groove of it and keep going, and I did not want to do that. So, although I might've slowed down, I wasn't going to just stop and quit. I was going to keep on working. My family was also there too. If I didn't have their support for what I was doing, even though they couldn't see a finished product, they said, "You got to get that done." My mom in particular was one of my biggest fans you know. She would just say, "Well, you know you got to get it done; you can't do anything else until you get it done." That's how she was.

Greta also found that her mother was a wonderful cheerleader for her. Her classes and dissertation required her to travel to the city where her mother lived, so even though she had to leave her husband and children to travel, she had a new home away from home:

It wasn't easy to delegate everything. My mom was a big cheerleader to get done, and in fact, probably she was my best, my biggest cheerleader. Because I stayed with her. She lives in Boston, and during the summers when I used to go there, I'd stay with her; every time I went there, I always stayed with her; so she was sad when I was done. She still says, "Well, I miss you coming up all the time. I really see you working at the university here." I said, "Mom, I'm not gonna work there. I don't want to commute anymore." But she was always there to listen, you know—she would feed me. I had a nice safe place to go to.

When Joanne began doctoral studies, she was still living at home and found that her parents did not understand why she would want to uproot herself to begin something as intensive as a long doctoral program. They did not understand her desire for advanced education:

I came from a small town. My mother had a ninth-grade education, my father had a seventh-grade education, and it was important to them that their children be able to have enough education to be able to make their way in the world. And so when I got my bachelor's degree they were very pleased. . . . And so there wasn't the value of advanced education—you have to be able to make your way in the world, and so you have enough education to make your way in the world; why would you want more education? And in fact, when I was accepted to the doctoral program, my mother said, "Why, I can't even imagine why you would need more education; you would have enough by this point in order to get a good job." Education itself was valued, but advanced education was not. And I didn't have the self-confidence: I had rarely been out of Georgia. Not that I was unwilling to try new things, but, you know, most of my family was still in that area; so it wasn't like I had great ambitions to move across the country. So I guess, some of it was self-confidence, some of it was the value of education, some of it was just fear of, you know, moving and you know, what it would be like to move that far away.

Bubbles shared a fun story of how her extended family viewed her research. As the first in her family to even go to college, her family could not understand her dedication to research on the mating habits of insects, and her grandmother thought there might be more important things a young woman could be doing:

I'm the first person in my family that's ever gone to college. So they had no idea, really (laughs), what I was doing. It was kind of this black box scenario for them. I know they knew that I worked a lot, and for me, that became an issue. . . . But they were very supportive. I have a funny story about my grandmother. So, I was out collecting insects for my work that I was doing, and I went over to her house, and I had my nets and everything, my stuff, and I said, "Hey Grandma, can I poke around in your bushes looking for my insects?" And she said, "Well, that's one way to spend your time." (laughs) That was her, like, why don't you have kids, I mean this was all the subtext I was reading into it, here's all the things you aren't spending your time on—having children and doing things that normal people do. So I always laugh at that.

Bubbles continued with an incident that happened one day when she rode up to the gas station on her motorcycle to look for bugs in the bushes:

> My cousin owned a gas station, and I would come in there, and there's like, a lot of gas stations attract—in the mornings there's always like two or three dudes that are just hanging out, like shooting the breeze before they head off to work or whatever, so I would go in there in the morning and get gas or get coffee, and they would be in there and my cousin would say, "Oh, there's Bubbles, she's the one that watches bugs fuck." (laughs) That was the description of what I do for a living. So I would just laugh and say, "Yeah, that's me," and that didn't really bother me, 'cause I just felt like, they don't know, it is so far removed from their—as one of my friends said, that is some rarefied fucking air that you are breathing there. Because you're just in so—I mean, who does that? Nobody in the real world has any concept that you would be watching insects have sex, and that this is something that people would ever do. So I always took it in the absurd way that I imagine I would take it, too, if I didn't know. And I just laughed about it.

Bubbles then added a touching comment that suggested how pleased she was that even though her father might not really understand her research, he understood that it was important to her:

> My dad loves science, and he's very—I mean he didn't go to college or anything, but he's very interested and was very, very proud.

Even though children at home meant that the household was more complicated to manage, women often talked about how they gained support from their children. Alecia found that the time she needed to spend with her son on his own activities was actually a help to her:

> I think I was very fortunate because I've always had a very strong network of family and friends and people. So I know being a parent, I was very grateful for having my son because it meant that

I wasn't totally consumed by graduate work. I had to do homework every day and play soccer and all these other things that make you balanced and healthy.

Celeste shared that although her husband meant well in trying to support her, it was her daughter who seemed to be able to sense what type of support she needed. When asked if she got support from her family, she noted:

My children more than my husband (laughs). My daughter is very good—*there's* a woman—[She says] "If there's anything I can do to help you"—or "Have you heard anything lately?"—but very general. Whereas he'll go "What's the latest—what have you heard from so-and-so?" "Well this deadline is coming up, what have you done with it?" . . . So he's a little more specific and a little more pressure I think. But it's just a man. But I know he's supportive. . . . As it was getting so frustrating, [my husband] George was saying, "Look, you don't need all this. If you're going to have exactly the same job and exactly the same position, then don't kill yourself worrying about this." But I feel that my children are just so proud that I've gone all the way through, and honestly, my son talks all the time about going on with his PhD, so maybe, that will be my legacy . . . will be my children continuing their education. It's never too late! (laughs)

Kim, a single mom, had to be on call at her company 24 hours a day but had no office and needed a place where she could work during quiet times at night. Her sons sensed her need and banded together to help her carve out and furnish a space at work where she could write:

I wasn't given an office by my department, so I found one. And it was a closet, a linen closet and my sons and I converted it, and it turned out to be a pretty neat place. I had a couch that was so comfortable. So I would write and spend the night. I would get up and finish something. You know how ideas come to you? And I would just rewrite it and rewrite it until I thought it was presentable.

Friends and Co-Workers

The women's stories made it clear that it was not that they needed one person for support; they needed a village—a trusted circle of friends and co-workers to help them deal with the stress. Interestingly, none of the women talked of a support group of men, or even groups that were composed of both women and men. All of the peer support people were women. It appeared that their women friends had a special way of knowing how to be helpful—sometimes just listening, sometimes giving advice, but always making them believe that they could succeed. Louise talked to the researcher about the type of support she received from her women friends:

> *Louise:* As women, my friends were very, very encouraging. Sometimes they would, like, baby me and things like that—even if I knew they were lying to me, they said, "Oh this is great, I'm so proud of you." (Laughs) And it's just so good to hear it sometimes, you know.
> *Researcher:* And is that mostly what support meant for you, saying "You're doing well and we're with you"?
> *Louise:* Yes, lying to me. (Laughs) No. Um, yes, that I was going to be done.

Suzy talked about a time when she felt immobilized with her dissertation, not being able to go forward, until she realized the value of surrounding herself regularly with her women friends:

> I knew I had to write. My advisor kept emailing me, "Where is Chapter 2?" That kind of thing. But I felt like I don't even know what to write. I'd sit at the computer with a bunch of reference articles feeling like I don't know where to go, I don't even know how to organize this. What am I writing? . . . And then I had a couple of my colleagues come over, and we had coffee, and we just talked, and we laughed a lot about our advisors, and somehow talking about it that afternoon, I thought, you know we're professionals, we're friends, we're *smart women*, we can do this. We know what we're doing. We can do this. And I think we

helped each other. So after that, we set a time to meet in a coffee shop once a month, and we would quiz each other on candidacy questions. And that was very helpful. That was really, really helpful. We would spend a couple of hours there and close down the shop. You know, I didn't feel alone. We would go home from there and say, yes, yes, I can do this.

Audrey found a different way to access a support group of women through participating daily in a video website where each woman supported the others in the thinking and writing process:

For most of my dissertation, I lived on video cam. Absolutely—especially in the last push. They were all women that were writing dissertations at the same time. I met them on a website which supports people writing dissertations. And we found a corner of that website and wrote every day, checked in every day, and talked about what we were doing, and encouraged one another, and this progressed into working by video, with—picture two girls, one in sociology, one in English—and we were—I was in Cincinnati, and one was in Santa Barbara and one in Canada. . . . When we were pushing to get finished, we were all doing it at the same time, and we would ritually check in at 9:00 in the morning and start the video, and this would run for 14 hours, 20 hours, until the last of us went to bed, and then, we'd get up and do it again. I wrote most of my dissertation by video chat, and I don't think I would have been able to do it otherwise. . . . And I don't know that I would have gotten up in the morning and gone and done it, but I knew that nine in the morning, the other two would be on and would be waiting for me, which meant trouble if I didn't turn up! (Laughs)

Joanne found that exercising with a friend who was also writing a dissertation gave her much-needed intellectual and emotional support:

I had a friend who was in the same—we'd been progressing through the program at the same pace, and so she was also working on her dissertation. And so [we] would get up in the morning and go to the park and run together and talk about, you know, a host of things, commiserate about where we were or were not in terms of input from our faculty advisors and the progress we were (laughs) or were not making. So having that kind of support network was helpful.

Callie talked about how "opening out" to her friend helped her:

Another PhD student whom I know was really, really supportive in that time. And I think often when you do open yourself out, that you can get back, it's a giving and receiving. You don't feel so much on your own, with how you feel. . . . So actually I think having that disclosure that, you know, "I'm feeling like I really can't cope," and hearing "I feel the same way," it sort of relieves a lot and makes you realize, maybe, you're not as abnormal as you perceive yourself to be. Maybe, I'm not so much of a failure. Because that's how I felt, that they see me as, "Oh, what's to be done?" You know, thinking, "She just can't even cope with it." . . . Because it was all-consuming. And I think it should be all-consuming. But, there's that keeping the balance.

It appeared that the participants' own success in their support group also helped others in the group. Greta was happy that her ability to move along quickly in the dissertation process helped her friends who were also working on their dissertation that "took forever":

And so, quite honestly, it was real interesting, the dynamics within the college where I work is that all of a sudden—"Greta, she started way after everybody else, but My God! She's pullin'"—I'm a race horse, ya know, and they're—I'm leaving them in the dust. So I was really a stimulus for two more of my faculty members to get finished since and one more to get started, and in fact, it's interesting 'cause one of my friends that's getting started, she says "I'm role modeling myself after you, Greta."

Mary wanted to make sure that her dissertation was a quality one so she found her own reviewers, in addition to her doctoral committee members:

> I had three people outside of the school—I actually sent the 200 pages to them, and they actually read the whole thing and sent it back to me. Because I wanted to make sure that . . . not that [my chair] would do this, but I wanted to make sure that I wasn't just being pushed through, and that my book product was . . . was good. I just wanted to make sure it was really good, and that some really critical people would never let me get by with anything but a good work product. They would have called me up and said, "This stinks," if it was bad. And I got good feedback from them, so that was a really, really big help, and it wasn't time-dependent or anything. It was just to know that the three of them, big intellectual giants out there, cared enough to make sure that I was producing something decent.

Since many of the women had paying jobs, in addition to writing a dissertation, their work environment was an important source for supportive relationships. Alecia talked about how the support of co-workers was important to her:

> It was nice having a group of people you're kind of in the trenches with, and you build relationships, and so it was nice having people who were asking me, "So what's your area of research?" . . . the talking in general, and I think that was very helpful because it was on a day-to-day or week-to-week kind of basis, where you came in and people said, "How are you, how's such-and-such going?"

Mary was moved at how her boss went to bat for her at a critical time:

> We had all these huge meetings, all this end of the year stuff, and it was just a ton of responsibility that I was supposed to do, but I had to take this time off, or I wouldn't finish. And [my boss] said to me, "Well, a year from now, I don't suppose anyone's going to remember that you weren't at the kick-off meeting for our national

Realigning Relationships

program, but I'm pretty sure a year from now, a lot of people will remember if you don't graduate with this doctorate." And he goes, "We put a lot of time into you—you take the time you need, you need two weeks, you take what you need to." And that was like totally overwhelming.

Naomi also found that the support of her boss helped tremendously at a critical time in the dissertation process:

When it got really bad, I almost quit. When one committee member, I can remember, was asking for the data analysis for the ninth time, and when my chair told me I had to do it. I told her on the phone—I started crying. And I told her that I quit. I told her, "You know what, I'm not doing it. I just, I give up." And then she said, "Well, think about it." And I was like, "You know I'll think about it," but I said, "I really, really, really want to quit!" And so I went and talked to my boss about it. . . . And he said, as comforting as he could, "Naomi, just do it. Just do whatever they ask you to do. Try not to complain about it, just get it done, get out, do what you want to do."

Celeste had the opposite experience with her supervisor compared with Mary and Naomi. While teaching in a college, she was completing a dissertation with a university 900 miles away, doing most of the work by email but also taking trips periodically to meet with her advisor. She felt that she got no support from the dean at her workplace:

Honestly, there's not a lot of love lost between me and my dean. And so I, because he's the academic dean, I've been to him on more than one occasion, and it's just he always works the conversation around to something else. And I've told him very specifically, I don't want to—I'm not going to be here that much longer. It's not a salary increase. I make already—because I've been here long enough—all I want is an "atta girl." And I mean, make me assistant professor at least. And it's just, it's awful. It's very demeaning. And it's frustrating and there's no one to talk to about it. It's very frustrating. It's very disappointing. Because one day at lunch, he goes, "Well have you all had a good week?" And my colleague goes, "Well Celeste actually got in two chapters." And he says, "Oh really, are you still doing that?"

Alecia found the competitiveness of the doctoral program led her to mistrust some of her peers:

There was a lot of competition in the doctoral program. And so, I had relationships, and a few really good . . . supportive . . ., but there were a lot of people who weren't that way . . . and who were just more competitive. . . . I'm not really like that, I mean I want to do well, but it's not like I'm worried about what you do. So, in terms of that, I was not used to people . . . I mean I had one person actually tell me the wrong thing on an assignment. Awful kinds of stuff.

Callie was shocked to find that one of her colleagues criticized her for being happy at accomplishing something she felt was important. She appeared excited that she could engage the researcher in telling her story:

Can I tell you something, actually? It's only because I think this is really—this has just really happened, and I think this is an important part of the developmental part of the relationship with friends . . . I did a couple of presentations about my work, and got validation. And people coming up saying, or emailing me, "Your work is fantastic." And it's just like, "Oh, God! All this time on your own, and then this has happened in a short period of time." And I was telling a friend of mine that things have been fantastic and really good. And she said, "Are you not getting a bit too big for your boots?" which I found—oh my God!—you know, and it started again, I thought I couldn't even be proud of what I did, outside of the circle, because it was perceived badly . . . And I was thinking, she knows how awful I was feeling a few months ago, and how awful it's been, and she knew I was having a really bad time—it was really hard to hear, and then to say—God, I can't even share . . . I think, definitely, that comment has stayed with me, really, and I've thought so much about it—about getting too big for my boots—it's made me think, kind of a lot—because I know I'm changing, and it just worried me.

As Callie continued with her story, it was evident that she was conflicted in her thinking about wanting to share new insights and intellectual ideas with her friends but also worried that the dissertation process had changed her and her relationships—perhaps permanently:

> I don't know if it makes much sense, really, because I think it's just such a fundamental—that's a word that's used a lot, but fundamental change in your life, that you do worry about how far it's changing, and realigning all parts of your—and maybe that's why that for some people, you have moved away perhaps intellectually as well, like I was saying before, there are conversations that I can't have anymore because I want to have ones that are more meaningful, because that's where I'm at. A few months ago, there was one night where I went to a dinner party with a group of friends, and I was really screaming, you know, I was, just inside—I can't bear this. So it does worry me, it does worry me. I don't really know if there's an answer to that in the long run. But right now I'm in this process, and, it's, you know it'd help to think not, because I don't want to be friendless you know, and, so it's awful to—I'd hope that I wouldn't be. I'd hope that, you know, it's about me establishing different relationships or seeing people for what they are and not what I am because I have changed, I have changed, and hopefully it isn't . . . I don't know, I hope I don't resent myself, I don't know, it's difficult to find the words—to not want to stop a relationship, getting to where I can still have a relationship with people that I have known and grown up with even though I feel like I'm in a different realm at the moment. But you know, obviously, I want to still work at keeping them close. My girlfriends are very important to me, there are certain things that happened in my life, that—they've supported me through a hell of a lot, and I would hate to—you know, stop through doing this. It certainly is a fear, a fear that I definitely feel that I might alienate them. And you know with [my partner] Joe as well—you know, it's scary. The whole thing of it is scary.

In summary, it was clear from interviews with the women in our study that their dissertations were often a life-changing process that intensely affected relationships with family, friends, and colleagues. Greta's comments clearly reflect this:

Life things happen—my mother had some serious health problems, my father-in-law—my son had a major injury. I had some hard times, but ya know—life happens. And that's one thing that I think is very hard about doctoral studies—is life happens. I think I was blessed during the dissertation writing phase. I had so many friends that I stayed in contact with. I had friends that were within the community where I live, that were working on—in the same path; maybe, I was a little bit ahead or I was little bit behind. So I was well supported, and what I see so often—and that's why I really seek out doctoral students. It doesn't matter what venue I'm in. And I try and support 'em. . . . You need cheerleaders and that's when all the supports disappear.

Kim also provided a moving summary of what a friend's support meant to her whenever she needed help

She was the one that gave me a glimpse that, maybe, I could do this . . . I mean, you bring back tremendous memories of, you know, I wasn't out there by myself. Yes, and I think each individual, everybody has their own barriers. And the way they choose to go over or around or under those barriers is going to be different, completely different from person to person. But for me, it was finding people and resources that would help me. So I think the only thing I really did was say, "Help!"

Reflections on the Stories

As we listened to the women's stories about their relationships, it was clear that these were *women's* stories, filled with the kind of knowing and unknowing that women encounter in their roles as wives, mothers, daughters, sisters, and friends as they grow and change. The stories were told, to use Carol Gilligan's phrase, "in a different voice"[1]—rich in descriptions of how these women relied on caring relationships and even structured and restructured these relationships to move forward to the goal of completing the dissertation.

Although it was clear that the women in our study often found comfort in their relationships with family and friends, their stories indicated that they often needed to realign these relationships in the context of their doctoral experiences. Family members and friends to whom our research participants had turned for support in past contexts suddenly did not seem to understand what was needed, and worse yet, the participants sometimes realized that the previous relationship did not work; they needed a type of relationship and dialogue that was different from the past, that would reflect the new perspectives they were gaining from their dissertation work, and from the demands and personal growth that accompanied that work.

The same learning process that helps women move toward successful completion of the important goal of their dissertation can threaten their long-established relationships. This phenomenon is similar to one Mary Catherine Bateson called "the strangeness hidden in the familiar":

Wherever lives overlap and flow together, there are depths of unknowing. Parents and children, partners, siblings, and friends repeatedly surprise us, revealing the need to learn where we are most at home. We even surprise ourselves in our own becoming, moving through the cycles of our lives. There is strangeness hidden in the familiar.[2]

Bateson suggests that the best friendships and relationships are those that "float" and have a degree of mystery, demanding growth and change to regain the intimacy that has disappeared in the relationships that move between strangers.[3] As the quality of intimate relationships is very important to women, they must be aware of the need to let these relationships "float" through change and growth, as each woman, herself, changes and grows. Perhaps the very experience of encountering conflicts in relationships as a result of the intense dissertation process can help women move forward toward newly intimate relationships with others to experience the wisdom that is born from the overlapping of lives.

In struggling to find what they themselves need in these realigned relationships, dissertation writers may also want to reflect on how their work affects the lives of life partners, family, and friends, and how their work even affects the very possibilities contained in those shared, overlapping lives. Alfred North Whitehead asks us to understand our world as a series of relations that are always in process.[4] There is no established future already existing, waiting to happen. Instead, each living creature, each rock, each particle in this world is connected to every other, directly or indirectly, and each is in process, changing at every moment. As a result, each of us, through our actions or inactions, affects the possibilities available for the next moment of the world. A person is unlikely ever to know how her choices affect plants or animals on the other side of the globe, but certainly, she can see how her choices affect the possibilities open to those she shares her life with. A marriage that suddenly has one partner devoting time to a dissertation has a changed set of possibilities—not necessarily inferior ones but possibly more limited. Likewise, a friendship's possibilities are changed and limited by the dissertation as the writer has little time to go out and have fun or is distracted when she does.

Whitehead and other process-relational philosophers argue that if we can see the world in this way, our motivation whenever possible should be to act in such a way that we might increase and enrich the possibilities for the world and for those around us as each overlapping moment comes into being. For a student writing a dissertation, that work itself may open up marvelous new possibilities for herself and her family, as she finds herself qualified for new career opportunities or discovers a new love for research and scholarship. But at the same time, other possibilities may be temporarily or forever closed off.

Some realigning of relationships during the dissertation is likely inevitable. In navigating and nurturing these realignments, dissertation writers may want to consider: What constitutes emotional support from my life partner and friends? How do I articulate the nature of that support and my need for it? Might I seek friends or peers online for daily or weekly check-ins? Dissertators and their family and friends may want to explore together: What losses or closed possibilities are my loved ones experiencing? How might family roles or chores be altered (temporarily or permanently) to help the writer focus on her work? Can the dissertating student make regular, even if just monthly, dates with her friends to stay connected and get the support she needs? Readers with children may want to ask: Can I make my work a positive element in my children's lives in addition to the negatives? How can I help my children understand how to be supportive without burdening them unfairly? Ideally, exploring these questions and others, the dissertating student can work and talk with her partner, family, and friends to create and nurture possibilities for all of their overlapping lives.

Chapter 4

Transformation of the Self

> *I think for a while I went back and forth to feeling really stupid, like I can't believe I'm this stupid, how could I not know this, I thought I could write. I would vacillate between feeling stupid and then feeling better, like wow! Every milestone helped me think, I'm not that stupid ... There is a level of self-confidence, I think, that I have now that I didn't have before in believing that I really can, I really can achieve a big project, ... I mean it is a major accomplishment! ... It created in me, sort of a feeling of, wow, you really can do this!*
>
> — Suzy

The women's stories were filled with reflections on their personal relationship with the dissertation, almost as if the dissertation was embodied. It became a constant (although not always welcome) companion day to day, hour to hour, for months and years. The intensity and length of the time the women were dissertating was unanticipated for many of them. They talked about being "obsessed," "hysterical," and "compulsive" during the dissertation as they invested so much of their life in this one activity. Yet, as in Suzy's reflection above, they realized that the dissertation process, in many ways, had transformed them.

The Stories

Many of the participants had professional careers and were accustomed to balancing diverse responsibilities efficiently and effectively. Others taught or did other work part-time while dissertating. All seemed confident and committed in their non-dissertation work situations. The fact that, now, they found themselves adrift without a clear idea of how they were to complete the dissertation was a new and incredibly stressful experience for these women. They often talked of coming home in tears after encountering a problem with their doctoral advisor or some other situation—behaviors that were completely uncharacteristic and puzzling to them. The interview process itself seemed to be cathartic for these women as they dialogued with the researchers and reflected on their own relationship to the dissertation. They talked of the importance of knowing who they were and what they wanted to do with a PhD. They shared feelings of not being good enough to measure up to the standards of PhD requirements and the difficulties of balancing priorities to concentrate on such an intensive experience as writing a dissertation. And they talked about the transformation process that occurred for them, often unexpectedly, in writing the dissertation.

Knowing Oneself

It was clear from listening to the participants' stories that these women had reflected deeply about who they were and why they would want to start, continue, and finish a journey that ended with a goal as difficult as writing a dissertation. Celeste described how she started her journey just to try it out:

When I started the whole process, I wasn't thinking that I would go all the way through. I was going to take some classes and—I didn't start out with the end game in mind. I was going to take some classes because I had an empty nest, and I was going to fill some time and get some new ideas for my teaching and then I got too far to quit is kind of what happened. I'd committed enough that I wanted to keep going. And the classes were interesting and . . . I made great connections with other people. . . . And I think women, women see a purpose—like whether you have young children, no children, old children—no matter if you're 27 or 57, I think we set our goals, I think we're focused for the most part. And we want—we have our steps, and we want to make them, we want to click them off, and we want to keep on going, and we don't want to go back—well, *I* don't want to go back! That's me. I don't want to go back. I want to go forward!

Gabriella also started her PhD program without a clear understanding of what it would be like, but she knew herself well enough to know that she could set up a plan to succeed:

At the point in my life that I decided to go back to do my PhD, I was as much motivated by the fact that I wanted new doors to open as I was, by that I wanted to learn more about ethics because I was also interested in other things . . . [I had] a sense of the things that one needs to be able to focus, and for everybody it's a little different, but for me, it was a separate place and a particular time, and a plan, the plan for having to go about it.

Gabriella also knew that she needed to find a way to complete this goal that was important for her in a way that would fit with her personal situation—integrating it into her busy professional and personal life:

It takes a lot of time and a lot of concentration. I mean, you have to focus. You have to sit down with, block out all the things that are constantly in our lives, and make it happen, and you can't you know, you can't cut corners because you have to do it, you have to find the time, and it is hard. I was still trying to work most of the time I was doing the dissertation, I had kids at home, I mean it was a busy time of life. But I was determined (laughs) to finish it. And so I spent many a late night, early morning. I actually found the best time for me to work on my dissertation was very early in the morning. I used to get up at three-thirty in the morning and work from four 'til seven. And it was a good time for me because I could, there were no distractions, and I could focus better than I could eleven o'clock at night. So for me that was the most fruitful time, really early in the morning. I'd come home from work, play with the kids, get them to bed, go to bed, get up, get up early and write and work and then until it was time to get everybody up to go to school, and come to work again. You know, so it was a busy time, but it worked for me to have a particular time, and that was my time, and a particular place. In our house, we have an attic that I was able to convert into a little office, which was, you know, right there—so I could go up there at four o'clock in the morning—but was separated enough from the rest of the house, that if there were other things going on downstairs, I didn't even always hear them.

Greta had thought deeply about what time in her life would be the right time to start her doctoral studies. She knew she needed to make her studies fit within the context of her family responsibilities and decided that that meant finishing before her son was in high school. Greta knew she was an excellent planner and was intent on carrying out her long range timeline all the way to completion of her dissertation:

I had a friend who completed everything but her master's thesis and had children and never finished. So "done" was important to me. So, like when I got my master's, I planned my children and finished my master's thesis when my son was like two months old. But that was planned—to be done (laughs). To be done. And I planned my family. When I decided to go back to school, I decided—I had a timeframe in mind. I wanted to be done before my son was going to high school. Okay, so I did finish, . . . I had a timeline planned to myself because everybody told me that he needed—my family needed me more when they were in high school.

Greta knew her strengths and weaknesses well, and she was able to use this knowledge to help her move along quickly in the dissertation process:

I had a mantra: "focus, Greta, focus," . . . I had positive affirmative statements all over my house—"Dr. Greta spending time with her family at the lake." "Dr. Greta" meant I got my dissertation done. Enjoying time with my family at the lake meant that in my personal business, I was able to get, to make enough money to buy a home on the lake or whatever. I had like six goals all in one positive affirmative statement. And I had that for about maybe at least two or three years, . . . I like to have time with my family. . . . I like to have fun. And when I'm going to school, it's hard to have fun. . . . Oftentimes people take so long and it is so drawn out—so it was kind of like—"Go! Ho! Go! Bravo! Get it done! Rah! Rah! Shishboom-ba! Run for the touchdown!" You know, hey, let's throw a long pass—forget about this inch and inch and inch. I mean that's how it felt to me. I mean let's just throw the football. You know, the quickest way.

Greta did finish her doctoral studies, including the dissertation, in record time, and she reflected on this at her graduation:

I was real disappointed that [my advisor] didn't come to graduation, but Dr. X did, and I said to her as I was standing in line and there was like eight other doctoral students graduating—I remember I said to her, "I didn't know any of these other girls." And I said, "You know, I think something's wrong with me. I did things too easy." I said, as my son always says, "I got done in 3.7 years." And she said, "Greta, Greta, no. You are unlike most people. When you would tell me that you would do something by what day, you did. Every time you said you would do something, you did. You kept on track and focused."

Greta shared some aspects of knowing oneself that she felt were especially important:

Know yourself. Know what you need as a learner. So then you can make sure that you have what you need. You know, kind of being your own advocate . . . like, for instance, I knew that [my advisor] was not going to give me personal support, but I found other faculty that I knew would. Okay, 'cause I knew that about myself. I knew that I needed a lot of support. That's why I went to [a school in] Boston. My mother, I knew my mother would help me. That was my—another primary reason besides being, I thought a good fit, is because I knew my mom would help me. . . . When you're doing your dissertation, what do you need? Whether it be, "Do you need a nice place to work?" A lot of people don't think about, well, where am I gonna work on something that's going to take two years? "Do I have a place at home that's just mine? Do I have a clean corner? Or can I make a corner? Can I make an office where I can just leave all my stuff out that no one's going to be saying, 'Well, I want to use the computer. I want to use that.'" You know, you create the place to work. That's part of your tools.

Martha also took stock of her skills and set out on a doctoral journey that she carefully planned. Her organizational skills and matter-of-fact approach helped her to move along quickly:

Mine really was not a miserable experience, so I can't really relate. And I think a lot of it has to do with your attitude when you're going in. . . . You know, I had, I was excited to do it, I knew what I wanted to work on, I didn't have any of that, you know, indecision—I knew exactly what I was gonna do, and I got to work. So it was a fun—a great learning experience for me. . . . It was a hell of a lot of work! I decided that I wasn't gonna leave that to chance, that, you know, I was responsible for it, that I was gonna be in charge of my progression. It should be an exciting experience, not one that, you know, that's full of dread and somebody's gonna make them miserable. So, it really changed—it just colored my approach.

Mary knew that she had strong skills and determination that would ensure that she would succeed in the dissertation process:

I never, never, never thought that I wouldn't finish. I knew I was going to finish, I invested way, way too much of my life in it. There was just no way.

But she also knew her strengths and weaknesses and even though she was a good writer, she set as one goal for her dissertation that she would become a stronger writer:

In my work life, I love to write, and I can write . . . and a lot of people can't write. So, in work, in business, there's a lot of crummy writers. So I write executive briefs, two-page memos, big proposals, little proposals, analyses. . . . Everything I write, I get, "great job, excellent work, just the insight we needed, can use," or whatever, 'cause I spend the time, and I can write. So, I wanted someone who was going to be critical . . . and I wanted first to have my thinking clear and pushed a little bit. I didn't want to just go through the motions of a project, and then writing a paper and describing a project. I wanted some evaluation. I wanted some push on some things, and so she was a perfect chair for me because like just asking the questions. . . . She read a whole section and she said, "Explain to me how that is different from what you wrote on page 13. Could you explain that to me so that I can see, is it a complementary piece or are you just being redundant—figure it out." You know what I mean? And sent me back with whole chunks of stuff. She was willing to overlook my—she was able to treat me as a student and give me feedback and evaluation and critical review of things. And I really wanted that. She was able to add depth to the work that I had to get it to really the highest level that it was.

Callie talked about knowing herself well enough that she needed to produce a dissertation that was not just okay, but really well done—"worthy." Otherwise, she would feel like a "fraud."

Somebody said, about a year ago, that a bad thesis will stay with you forever. And it would for me—just on a personal level. That it will sit there and you'll always know. In fact, I think I'd feel like a fraud. If I got a PhD with a piece of work that didn't have the level that I felt . . . I'd feel like a fraud for accepting qualifications for something that I felt was sub-standard.

She also sensed that some of her personal qualities would help her succeed in this effort to produce a quality dissertation, not just because of her ability to write but because of her interpersonal skills that helped participants in her research trust her and share their intimate stories:

> I don't know if I'm a special person, but I think you need to have special qualities as a researcher—to a degree. I think there's a connection you can get with some that you just—I don't know, you can get on a level with somebody, can't you? Like I wouldn't say that with all the women I've met, but certainly with some, that there's some connection formed, and then, they say they are sure they can trust me. Which is a brilliant thing to actually hear about yourself. Even in an hour meeting, that they felt they could trust you with that information, that is very, very personal to them. . . . Maybe people think, you can get through a thesis, it's just standard; but it's not standard to me. And that's what makes it—I don't want it just to get through. I want it to be—because it's part of me, it's part of what I feel, I'm part of that work, worthy of the effort. And worthy of the women that I represent.

Kim felt that she was a very weak writer and worried about how, even though she loved research, she would complete the dissertation. Knowing her weakness, she strategized to make sure that she would have the necessary support for her writing that she knew would be above and beyond what her dissertation chair could provide for her:

> I have confidence in bread making. I can make bread. But I didn't have that same confidence in my writing ability, so I would seek out people who would give me an honest opinion, like for example, [my colleague], she didn't know anything I was saying she said, but she knew English, and she would correct my punctuation, or she would correct my tense, and that was incredibly helpful. And she would also correct my spelling even though I had spell check! (Laughs) And see, it not only takes a village to raise a child—all this is telling you how many people I involved in helping me get that ticket punched, it never is solely just one person.

Bubbles was the only woman in our study who started her dissertation at one university and then switched to another, which was the university where she had previously received her master's degree. Although she felt that she was doing good work on her dissertation, she kept asking herself whether it was really going to help her develop in her personal and professional life in the way she wanted and needed. She talked at length about the difficulty of making this decision but how important she felt it was to have made the decision that was right for her:

> Here's where the *not good* part is. I actually had started a PhD at another institution before . . . I was very well into it. I had done a lot of work. . . . I actually thought that the work was really good, and I was enjoying it, but the person that I was working for was just—crazy. He did not emphasize scholarship or going to meetings; he basically encouraged us not to go to departmental talks, it's just a waste of time if it's not the sort of narrow thing that you're working on—and that was completely antithetical to what my training before had told me, which was you will go to every talk. So it was this very different, opposed view, and I just didn't like it, I didn't agree with it. And the guy was kind of crazy, and we'd had a couple of run-ins, and then I just—I have a somewhat fiery personality (laughs) and there were a couple of other people there at the time, and we were all very unhappy. We called our office the den of despair. . . . It felt like I'm going to toil away here in obscurity and get no professional development, and then what am I going to do when I leave here? And that was the part that bothered me. I think the quality of my work was fine and it would have been fine, but it's always better when you have intellectual and emotional support—that's always better. But I had experience, so I probably could have done it and said, this is fine, but you work so hard, I mean working 70 hours a week, and then to say "It's fine," that's not satisfying, you know; it wants to be great, or otherwise it's not worth it. . . .
>
> And I spent two years there, and ended up leaving . . . I basically just realized that I wasn't going to have the career that I wanted to have if I stayed there. And I hadn't originally thought about going back to where I did my master's. I had talked to a couple of other people, but then, I had gone to visit my [eventual] PhD advisor

and his wife, and we were just talking about this crazy situation I was in. I was describing to them some of the things that were going on. And they were both just saying, "You've got to get out of there, you've got to get out of there." And none of us were really thinking at the time, you have to come back here. But after I just kind of started thinking, well, I spent two years here and really have very little to show for it, and here is a person that I have a great relationship with, and I know I can do good work with, and a place that I know is very productive and supportive, what am I doing, you know? Why am I just not there? . . . And so I decided to go back there, and, from then on, it was all good . . . I always did end up thinking I made the right decision. It was difficult, but once that move was made, from then on out, I felt very good about what I was doing and all the work that followed, so it turned out for the best.

Impostor Syndrome

As women struggle in the dissertation process with the pressure to produce quality research and writing amidst the many other priorities they face, they often experience self-doubt and begin to question whether they even belong in the doctoral program. Often called "the impostor syndrome," this state of mind can cause students to compare themselves unfavorably with others who they may see advancing faster in the program. Most of the participants in this study expressed feelings of impostor syndrome as they struggled to find *their* place in the world of accepted scholarship. Louise talked about how she would work tirelessly trying to produce a good paper for her committee:

I would spend hours and hours reading stuff, and I think I'm borderline ADD, so I can sit and read, and my mind goes in all directions. So I could read a paper 10 times, and I still won't catch all the mistakes. So with somebody else's paper it's different. Because I'm so nervous, it takes me a really long time to relax and calm down and really get my mind cool and everything.

She would tell her committee to expect the paper on a certain date so that they would have time to read it and would then despair if she was not able to meet the deadlines she had set for herself:

"Oh, I'll send you something this week, could you please read it before you go on vacation?" And you make sure, and then it's not ready. And you're like, "Gosh, they're going to give up on me."

As reflected in the epigraph at the beginning of this chapter, Suzy was mystified at her "feeling stupid" when she usually felt confident about meeting her goals. It appeared that the step-by-step process of creating the dissertation did give her new confidence, although she still needed the validation of her advisor:

Every milestone helped me think, I'm not that stupid, like finishing Chapter 1. My advisor would say, "Let's see Chapter 2." "Okay, let's go to Chapter 3." Every milestone helped me think, "Hey, I think I can, I think *I can* do this!" And then, ultimately, when I had data collected and analyzed *ad nauseam*, writing things out over and over again, when my advisor said, "I think we can set a date," I thought, "Hey, I'm not stupid!"

Stella felt that because her advisor did not seem very interested in her, it must be that the quality of her work was not good:

I just felt like she likes her other students better than me, she's giving all of her time to her other students, she must not be interested in my work at all. She must think my work is so boring. She doesn't want to spend any time on my work at all. And I think also something that happens in graduate school is that you work on something so long, and so intensely and so intimately that it's like things seem obvious and trivial to you, and you forget that no one else in the world feels that way about your topic except you. There's really not a single person that's going to look at your topic that you have spent the last three, four years thinking about, and go, "Oh yeah, that's obvious." But I think that's a problem for graduate students, and, you know, other people are experts, but I'm a student, and part of also writing my dissertation was that process of shifting that mental state. That transition from "I'm a student" to "I'm an expert in something." And so I almost feel like for most people, it can't help but be a scary feeling, that sort of shifting where, oh my gosh, I'm the one who knows the most about this? And then acknowledging that and, um, there's something very disarming about that, that shift.

Alecia was intimidated by the solo aspect of her dissertation. Even though she knew the committee needed to approve it, she still experienced anxiety from the feeling that it was hers alone to produce:

It is a very solo event, and ultimately it's you. Your name alone sits on it—and then you turn the page and find these other people, but some ways I think it's an interesting thing, that it doesn't feel it because you have all this committee and criticism and whatever, but ultimately it's very solo. I think it is very difficult when you think about the fact that you're set up on so many levels for student evaluations, peer evaluations, peer review of articles, peer review of . . . and your whole life is set up saying, "Here I am, now tell me everything I'm doing wrong." (Laughs)

Joanne shared how difficult it was for her to maintain her self-confidence in writing her dissertation:

There was nothing holding me back from a personal perspective; it was more of a not being confident that I had what it took in order to be able to do research. . . . It was something that sounds so simple in talking about it now, but just that discipline to force yourself to put the words on paper went a long way to actually getting through to completion. . . . And being the shy girl from Georgia, getting in front of the committee [for the defense] was not an easy thing to do.

Callie was almost finished with her dissertation during our interview but had not yet defended. She talked about how she did not feel like a real scholar even though she was doing many of the same kinds of things that she would do after she finished her PhD:

I'm a fake academic! I do, I feel like when I'm speaking at this conference, at the moment—I feel less confident about talking in academic circles because I feel I haven't got a true voice, without having gone through the process. . . . Doing a PhD, you just lose all that validation that I used to have within—I worked as a manager for five years and had loads of validation because I was well respected and I was very, very productive. Signing things off every day, a hundred emails, doing this, doing that, but doing your PhD—that's another thing.

The advisors' and committee members' responses to manuscripts were taken very seriously by all the participants, and criticism was often hard to accept. Greta talked about how negative feedback affected her self-esteem:

Fragile?! Well, you know, if you define yourself by what you are and what you produce, you go into a meeting and people say, "This is shit. This is awful." . . . You go in thinking you gave it your best work. . . . So, ya know, your self-esteem is tied up with that, and so somebody says you didn't do a good job—your self-esteem is very fragile.

Greta knew that her advisor wanted her to be confident, even amidst the criticism she received from the committee, so she remade herself to appear that way:

Every time I went to [my advisor], I put on my persona. She did not want to hear about how I didn't know how to do things. I could not appear like I was clueless. So I came just the way I teach people to go to the doctor's office. I came with my list of questions, I was organized, I was methodical, and she'd say, "What do we need to talk about today?" And I had it all outlined, right there in front of me—dut, dut, dut, dut. I was very organized. And I looked like I was—I faked it. And I did it with some suggestions from some of my friends, so I was the confident researcher. I didn't show my weak side.

The audience is important for any writer, but Eleanor talked about how imagining an audience of scholars reading her drafts, specifically the committee, created feelings of self-doubt that led to writing blocks:

> One thing I've noticed as I'm writing, that one thing that holds me back, that gets me stuck is when I start envisioning who the audience will actually be as the people on the committee. And the view I attribute to the people on the committee even though I would say this is a reflection probably of my fears and not—there's been no indication at all that this is their view—so it's probably my fear. My fear is that the view of the people on the committee is that this is an evaluative tool to see, do we think you have the chops to be one of us? Are you good enough to be part of this club?

Eleanor even thought about how her visits to her advisor's office added to her self-doubt. As she talked about this with the researcher, however, she concluded that it was not the advisor's office itself that was intimidating, but how it represented the power of the academic community:

> *Eleanor:* One thing I've probably been doing is thinking of the advisor's office as part of that. The advisor, as well, is making evaluations and coming to a determination of whether or not—not only the work itself but whether or not you as a person have the skills and qualities to justify your being seen as a faculty person.
> *Researcher:* So meeting with an advisor in his office, it sounds like it connects him with all of that institutional, academia stuff? And that's where the intimidation is coming from, is that right?
> *Eleanor:* Yes, in part. I think the other part is kind of the fake sense of security that it's tempting to derive from what already has been put forward—you're identifying a new idea and trying to look at it in a new way and hopefully move beyond just what is already in place in the machinery and just kind of break free of the machinery, it's sort of

a reminder that this machinery has a lot of power. It can get you jobs, it can get you acceptance, and so there's a lot of temptation to sort of succumb to that, rather than, maybe, taking a less safe route that actually would be closer to discovery and the kind of process I think, in my heart, we're hopefully called to do if we're really trying to pursue what we believe is valuable. So it's not that the advisor himself is intimidating or that they're intending their office to be intimidating because I find my advisor's office was actually constructed so as *not* to be intimidating. There weren't lots of degrees hanging on the walls, there wasn't any formal furniture, there were many personal items around, there wasn't an attempt to sort of screen out, or "look at my good taste," or "look at all the intellectual things I'm involved in." It wasn't anything like that, but I still have that reaction. And I don't believe it was from anything he was intentionally putting out there.

In thinking about writing her dissertation, Gretchen remembered how earlier in her doctoral program one of her professors encouraged her not to question her ability:

I had a graduate professor in a class . . . and he was in the School of Business. And I turned in this *great* paper, and I did everything I knew I was supposed to do, and he just looked at it, and he looked at me, and he said, "*Why* do you . . . think that you have to work so hard! This is fantastic!" (Laughs) And, like, and then I didn't know quite what to think about that, but I understood what he was saying because he said, "You know, it's okay. You *are* good." And I think that's what the message that I would give to people, that you *are* good. Get over this "less than" mentality.

Audrey's story illustrates how the intense dissertation process can threaten the self-confidence that students may have when they enter the program, leading to self-doubts about their success. For her, this lack of confidence caused her to obsess over details in her dissertation, but she finally convinced herself that, at some point, she would finish her dissertation—she would be successful:

> I think sometimes in the first period, it was still in the back of my mind as a possibility, that this wasn't going to get done, that I wasn't up to it, that I would never be able to finish it, that it would take me years and years and I'd be a disgrace to the department, and you know, I was plagued with the feeling that I was much worse than everybody else who was in the graduate program, that kind of anxiety that I had. But when I was doing it so intensely, it hit me at some point, this is going to get done! And I'm going to pass! It is strange, but I'd never had that before, I certainly didn't have it going in—well, maybe I had it going in, but after a year or so (laughs), . . . It was very real to me that this might be something that would never get done, and I was wasting my time, wasting my life. But when it came down to that push, even if it was a long way off, there was an end in sight, and that end was a successful end.

Gabriella summarized how she balanced her feelings of not being good enough with the realization that she just needed to finish the job well:

> I had good advice from somebody along the way—that it is important to do it well, but it is more important to get it *done* well because it's not like it's your life work. This is the *beginning* of your life's work. So do your dissertation, do it well, but get it done . . . and I always kept that message in mind. There is, there is a risk, especially for people who like to do things well, that you can never think it's quite good enough. And there's a point at which you have to say, look, it's good enough, it's going to be good enough. And somebody else judges whether or not it's good enough. And my committee was very helpful in that regard.

Balancing Priorities

Although anyone who writes a dissertation needs to do it while balancing other priorities, the women who shared their stories in this study talked about their priorities in a way that appeared to be directly related to their gendered role in society—as mother, daughter, wife, sister, employee. Louise talked with the researchers about how the stress of balancing priorities for family and career in the midst of writing a dissertation caused her to obsess about using every minute of time productively:

> *Louise:* The stress. You know about it, but you don't think it's going to be all the time, pretty much all the time. And even when you think you're not stressed, you are. It's something that sneaks up on you all the time. I think I did a decent job balancing because my husband was good at helping me. I mean he's done this before, and I can count on him for house cleaning and a lot of house chores. And I have to be organized, and it's something; otherwise, I wouldn't have been able to do . . . I was stressed all the time, 'cause I had to work, drive, and do the dissertation . . .
>
> *Researcher:* And what is it that you're balancing?
>
> *Louise:* Your private life and your career. Everything. You have to balance all that. For me it was hardest to plan family visits. You don't, you want to know everything ahead so you can plan your life. Every single hour counted for me . . . one hour could be a lot of reading, a lot of notes, or "I can correct 10 pages!"

Callie was used to thinking of herself as "super-woman," but in the process of writing her dissertation, she came face-to-face with the reality that she wasn't "okay":

A few months ago, I had a really bad time, and in fact, kind of a surprising time for me. I think I was under pressure, and the lack of validation, and I think my life had changed so fundamentally. From holding a position and being part of a team, and all this, and then coming back to being a lot more of a mom and kind of having to be centered on the kids and having to find a way to make this thing fit in around—a completely different life. And I felt very embarrassed because [my committee] knew I wasn't okay. And I ended up saying I wasn't okay. And that was an awful thing for me because I feel like I'm super-woman. You know, I've worked, studied, and taken care of my kids for years. I've always juggled really well—it sounds like, well, I probably am very needy to a degree. I needed some validation of who I was. . . . Any free time was my dissertation, that's my focus, to do, all toward the same goal. So if I sat in the car, I'd be reading. You know, as soon as the kids have gone to bed, I'm reading, working. So I was trying to cram everything in 'til having that kind of point where it was like, "It can't continue because what's going to happen if I continue the way that I am?" . . . And trying to add something on top that means the world to me at the moment, you know, it's 90 percent of my focus, really, and I sit with the kids, and I'm writing notes, and . . . so it's balancing. Balance is a really significant part in lots of ways.

Bubbles had thought deeply about setting priorities because, during her master's program, she realized that she was not balancing her life well:

You're going to go through the roller coaster and the ups and downs of every day, sort of thinking, what am I doing? And you just have to let yourself off the hook a little I think. And I had already done that because I had been, having gone through a master's, that's where I really effed up because I threw over my entire life to that, and my dad became very ill, and even though we were in the same place, he called somebody else to go to the hospital. And I really just had this realization then—what am I doing? When I'm sitting on my big mountain of whatever, alone, because I have alienated everyone because I'm a workaholic, what is that going to do for my life? And so by the time I got to my PhD work, I tried to be as balanced as a person can be, which is—there's always pressure from everyone in this culture. It's like a machismo thing, like (puts on deep voice), "I was in the lab 'til ten o'clock last night, and I didn't sleep at all." Well, I don't find that very compelling because I know that the work I do is better when I do have sleep and when I do have a chance to rest my batteries, so you have to really fight against those people and that type of culture. I felt okay doing that.

Greta found herself balancing her dissertation process with her family obligations in an unexpected way:

I remember defending my proposal. I thought it was no big deal. So I went to the meeting like "Okay just like another little meeting." . . . Well, I was on the ninth floor talking about my proposal, and the fire alarm went off, and my children were there with me 'cause we decided to enjoy Boston that day . . . and all I could worry about is, "Oh my God, where are my kids!" 'Cause this is in the middle of Boston, and they were on the ninth floor, and fire alarms were going off—the fire alarms had never gone off in three years! So I was very worried. So I mean it just kinda like put it in context it—was just like "wow."

Although this incident was an unusual occurrence, it illustrates the ways in which a student can be taken off guard by a sudden need to place her dissertation in the context of family, or vice versa.

Suzy, who had eight children and a husband whose job failed during the period when she was writing the dissertation, talked about how the dissertation was always with her as she balanced her academic, personal, and family life. Her dissertation was on the importance of light for healing, and even at her daughter's wedding she found herself thinking she should write down the sudden insights she got about how light might be affecting the wedding party:

The dissertation was hanging over your head, every day, every hour. I had two daughters that got married during the process—weddings, debts, illnesses, things I had to deal with—just trying to deal with regular life that is often unplanned. And then having the pressure of trying to complete this research project on top of it. It wasn't the pattern that I set out to do when I first started. But talking to others, other colleagues that I went through school with, we all had things that happened, you can't go through life for 4–5 years without things happening. . . . When you're in the middle of something like a dissertation, it's always, always over you, it's always there. You think about it in the night, you think about it on vacation, you think about it at your daughter's wedding, you think about it all the time. You find yourself at a restaurant with friends, getting out a paper and pencil because you had a thought about this. It's ever-present with you. . . . I remember my daughter's wedding, it was a beautiful venue at the country club. (Laughs) And as the sun was setting, I was thinking about how the light circadian rhythm in the summer—she got married in June—is affected. As the sun was setting over this beautiful golf course, I was thinking, "Circadian timing really may influence how people feel at a wedding." It's always with you!

The pressure of constantly trying to fit the dissertation into very busy personal and professional lives created intense stress for the participants. Callie described how the intensity of the process was greater than anything she had ever experienced and caused her to see herself in relation to her family in a new and sad light. She began to resent her situation:

I think I was starting to feel really devalued with the family, you know, being this kind of mom at home, which I've never been. And of course I love my kids dearly, but I'm not one to stay at home with the kids all day. And I was finding that I was having to do— and I have two young boys and an older daughter, and it's hard. You know, the hard work and the fighting, and having to deal with that all on my own, because Joe's gone off to work, and he just gets himself dressed. There was a lot of resentment. And then I feel like I have to make tea, and I have to do this and that—

Nothing else has affected me I think as—and I've done counseling work. But kind of the deepness of this, or the wholeness of this experience is—because everything's been pushed. Everything I feel like I've kind of known about the world—my relationships, my emotions, my capabilities—you know are kind of being shown to light to me, all of which is hard. . . . There are days—you know, there are moments that I have of this elation and a lot of bleak, kind of in-between, but at least I'm getting the elation. Which does fuel you on, absolutely.

Martha described how difficult it was to have to lead a normal life while balancing so much:

I mean, probably, the biggest barrier is how do you work full time and go to school and write your dissertation and still have time to sleep. So you try to balance all that, which is quite difficult, so it was literally my life for about 18 months.

Greta talked about the negativity that the dissertation brought forth, causing her to remove herself, she thought perhaps selfishly, from her daily responsibilities so she did not have to worry about contaminating her family:

You can be a negative influence. Oh, very, very negative. Oh yeah. And people don't like to be around you. So I would take myself away, really quite honestly, going to Boston because I could keep that world a little bit away from my everyday life. I worked real hard when I was gone, and then I could come home, and I could be more of a semblance of normal or whatever. . . . Quite honestly, I got to be very selfish. Because I only had to take care of me, and when you're having two kids and you're teaching, it was really a wonderful vacation. In fact, it was very hard when I stopped leaving 'cause I loved, 'cause it was one of my methods of coping with stress, was to leave. And when I was negative, I could leave. I didn't have to contaminate, and so that's why, so that's why I was very conscious of contaminating people is that when I'm now back and I'm having bad days, I'm contaminating (laughs). Whereas before, I could just leave, and they didn't have to put up with me, and I was by myself.

Transformation

In the end, it appeared that the dissertation process was a transformative experience for many of the women in this study, and in spite of many difficulties in the process, they felt that they had been changed. Gabriella talked about how she learned much from the process of her dissertation:

I learned a lot during my dissertation. . . . People think if that's right, you already know what you need to do, you just have to write it down. I don't think so. I really don't. I think doing your dissertation is a process of learning. And I actually, sure there were times when I wanted to pull my hair out and all that stuff, but there were times when I was really excited about what I was learning and then trying to, you know, digest, and put together into a coherent dissertation. And I learned a lot.

Eleanor noted that writing a dissertation had helped her realize how to meet other goals:

Whatever fears I've been carrying through the dissertation the past few years certainly have impacted the way I'll approach other goals.

Joanne described the benefits from the dissertation process simply as "more than the sum of the parts":

There's lots of, you know, back-and-forth, and you're so tired of revising and revising, and you think you've got it, and they want more changes, and so just being able to persevere through all of that and not have thin skin about the critique because that's their job—their job is to challenge you to think, their job is to think like a scholar—and you know, that doesn't happen without someone saying, "You know, your idea's half-baked." So you have to defend it, you have to be able to, you know, in a cogent way, make your argument for why you agree or disagree with the advice that's being provided by your mentors. And over time, you know, hopefully you've grown enough that you've become an expert in a particular area that is more than the sum of the parts.

Celeste stated that her goal was intellectual development even though that wasn't her original focus:

Intellectual development. It's become more personal. It's crazy. That's what my husband says, "You're crazy!" . . . I've become so much more computer savvy. I know more than anyone in the family. So that's been a plus . . . I think that I'm a little more creative in some aspects than I used to be just because of being exposed to some different things. And I guess, I'm a little more determined. I don't give up as easily. It used to be if I got frustrated, I would quit or just stop doing whatever. Now after working with whatever problems there were in my dissertation process, I have a little more patience with trying to work through things. I do because I've had to. And so that's been really good. That's good for me . . . I see it in other areas, the things that work if you try to put something together, working through projects; if it doesn't work the first time, you just try something else. So that's been better for me than just saying forget it, if it doesn't work easy, I'm not going to do it. So that's good. There have been lots of benefits.

Kim shared how a faculty member, who was not even associated with her dissertation, reached out to her because she knew that Kim had difficulty with writing and needed something to bolster her confidence:

She knew of my writing difficulties, so she had me write an article for her ethics forum, and she said, "We're going to do this together: I'm going to be the editor, and you're going to be the writer, and I will be with you." And that meant, that was my first genuine publication even though it was small. And that meant so much to me, that I could, with the august, world-wide person that she was, that I had my name next to hers.

Louise stated that the process of going through the dissertation made her realize some of her capabilities:

I have learned a lot about myself. . . . I've learned that doing a good job takes so much time. And you learn to be patient because it is something, part of the profession—we're working with time and thought processes. . . . You're actually learning your job, and at the same time, when you defend, you're being approved that you can do this because you did an okay job. You've learned to work by yourself, process information, write about it. . . . I know I'm not a good writer, so it wasn't like, "Oh I'm having a terrible day," it would be like, "Well, it's just going to be a day." And sometimes, it would be a lot easier, and I would be happy with what I would read, and it would be okay. I'm a decent writer, but I'm not like somebody who's really great, and suddenly, I'm having a bad day so—my strengths were being organized and making the reading interesting and organizing the dissertation and finding information. The writing, that's just the way it is, . . . I mean it's not great, but I have read pages of dissertations before—you know I would go to the shelves and look at some of my peers—it made me feel better, it'd be like, "Oh, she always gets prizes, let's see how she writes." And you read the introduction, and you're just like, "Boy, I can do better than that." And you feel so much better! I'm sure people will open mine and do the same! (Laughs)

In reflecting on her feelings about her advisor, Louise realized how she had grown to adulthood through the dissertation process:

I could tell the tone . . . and I'm like, "Can you just listen to me." So I think, I don't know—maybe it's also part of becoming adults, too, because for me, it was part of—I mean I wasn't an adult, fully adult I guess, when I started it. I still had a lot of personal issues and things like that. And I think a dissertation is—everything comes out because you have so much stress, and you have to sort out everything.

Callie summarized the insights she gained from the dissertation process through the vision of climbing slowly up a steep hill to arrive at a "completely different realm of understanding":

It is a huge, developmental process, the PhD, on many different— it's changed me . . . I think I see it as a vehicle, I see it as something that's occasionally a slow-moving vehicle for me, and it has all these little facets that are being pulled on, as if you're going up a hill perhaps, really. Starting from the bottom and then moving very slowly, as I'm trying to gain this knowledge and understanding. Because, for me, it's like I'm moving into a completely different realm of understanding . . . and I think I've come a long way, and I'm doing things I never would have done before. And yeah, it's good.

I certainly wouldn't want to be in any other place. I feel very privileged . . . I do think it's an absolutely transformative time in my life, you know, every which way—intellectually, emotionally, socially . . . I'm sure I'm changing, and I know things have changed, and I think something like that kind of sticks in more, doesn't it? Because you know yourself . . . this kind of self-actualization, or this, I don't know, absolutely overwhelming feeling of, "Oh my God, maybe I am worthy."

As Kim talked about the details of her research—defining the problem, collecting and analyzing the data, and finally discussing the conclusions and implications, she summarized the experience simply:

I think with the dissertation, as a process, that it really does teach you the research process, but it also teaches *you*.

Reflections on the Stories

We were amazed by these women as they told stories of how they moved through doubts of being competent to write a dissertation, found ways to balance daunting and competing priorities, and finally realized the important ways in which they were changed by the process. We believe that it is important for doctoral advisors as well as students themselves, to understand how the context of writing a dissertation can affect the sense of self of a student. In addition, there is likely a direct connection between the learning that occurs in the dissertation process and the changes in one's sense of self. As Mary Catherine Bateson explains, "In learning, one is changed, becoming someone slightly—or sometimes profoundly—different. What is learned becomes a part of the self, a part of that system of self-definition which filters all future perceptions and possibilities of learning."[1]

Bateson's phrasing here is similar to ideas expressed by existentialist philosophers, who argue that "existence precedes essence," that through our actions, through our daily lives, we create ourselves and create our own purpose and meaning. Jean-Paul Sartre explains it this way:

> Man first of all exists, encounters himself, surges up in the world—and defines himself afterwards. If man as the existentialist sees him is not definable, it is because to begin with he is nothing. He will not be anything until later, and then he will be what he makes of himself. . . . Not that he is simply what he conceives himself to be, but he is what he wills . . . as he wills to be after that leap towards existence. Man is nothing else but that which he makes of himself.[2]

With each decision we make or action we take, we create and shape ourselves. This realization that we have the power—even necessity—to create ourselves by our own design can cause great anxiety and disorientation,[3] and it may be that the "impostor syndrome" expressed by many of our participants is caused, in part, by such a realization. While the women in our study may not define their experience in existentialist terms, they were nonetheless on an existentialist journey in their dissertation process, struggling to find a new definition of themselves as scholars and writers. Students just embarking on such a journey may take heart in the existentialists' insistence that in defining ourselves, in choosing our own purpose, that definition and purpose are all the more meaningful, chosen deliberately and freely through a will to fulfill one's own possibilities.

In addition to being changed and redefining ourselves through our learning, something else more complex may be at play here. Edith Stein argues that each of us forms her sense of self partly from her inner perceptions and partly from her understanding of how others see her: "To consider ourselves in inner perception, i.e. to consider our psychic 'I' and its attributes, means to see ourselves as another and as he sees us."[4] When we have experiences, we are also often aware of how others perceive our experiences, and when we react to our experiences by displaying certain signs of our emotions, others' reactions to those signs become part of our experience.[5]

Because we are often or perhaps always in this kind of empathic exchange with those around us, the effects of this empathic feedback on our sense of self can be varied and manifold. Just as an object such as a jug can have "as many varieties of appearances as there are perceiving subjects," Stein says, "I can have just as many 'interpretations' of my psychic individual as I can have interpreting subjects."[6] As these interpretations of ourselves come back to us from a wide variety of people, we unconsciously compare them to our own self-perceptions. We may judge some to be false or incorrect, or we may adjust our own self-perception to bring it in line with others' interpretations of who we are. Stein believes we can all have strong inner perceptions of ourselves independent of others' perceptions, but empathy will always be an aid in comprehending ourselves because we allow for the possibility that another might judge us more accurately than we judge ourselves. As she says, "empathy and inner perception work hand in hand to give me myself to myself."[7]

For a student who is redefining herself as a scholar, who finds herself with entirely new peers and advisors reflecting their perceptions of who she is and how she experiences, this multiplicity of "interpreting subjects" can mean that she is constantly re-evaluating her inner perception of herself as she compares it with how others see her. This process may be disorienting and exciting at the same time. If the student sees herself as an impostor but senses her peers or committee treating her as a competent scholar, that mismatch in perceptions could add to her anxiety or help her correct her misperception of herself. If she embraces her identity as a scholar, she may encounter dissonance at home with her partner or children who see her as something primarily different, a wife or mother. But whatever the context, Stein would encourage these women to remember that inner perception and empathy must go hand in hand; while empathy and its conveyance of others' perceptions can be a comparative or a corrective to inner perceptions, each individual ultimately determines how to define her own sense of self from these multiplicity of interpretations.

Probably few students start a dissertation thinking about how the process will be transformative. Yet it was clear from the women in this study that they saw themselves very differently after completing this long and difficult process. In thinking about the effect of the dissertation process on one's own sense of self, readers may want to ask themselves: Why am I getting this doctorate? Do I really know that I'm good enough to do this, or do I feel like a fake academic? What strengths and weaknesses should I be aware of, such as writing, research, and interpersonal skills? How honest do I want to be about my sense of self with my family, friends, and advisor—do I need or want to put on a persona? How can I reduce the stress of balancing my competing priorities? What *is* balance in my life—where do I draw the line with too much sacrifice of time with family and friends? How have I changed by going through this process? Are there ways I want to change? Honest reflection on questions like these will lead readers toward Greta's advice: "Know yourself. Know what you need as a learner. So then you can make sure that you have what you need."

CHAPTER 5

ADVISOR AND COMMITTEE: DANCING WITH STRANGERS

> *I'd say, avoid mean people. That's it! I've made that a point in my life. I don't hang around with mean people! (Laughs) I, especially, don't want them on the committee because some people just take great joy in, you know, in tearing people down. So I don't want any part of 'em.*
>
> — Martha

There was probably no topic that was discussed more often by the women in our study than their committee. It was interesting for us to hear these stories as we each had our own memories of our dissertation committees but had thought of them as unique to our individual experiences. Listening to the stories of these women brought our own experiences back with fresh reality and made us realize that our remembered encounters and events were not unique. Many of the participants talked of their experiences in just the way we would have.

Some women described what they felt was an ideal relationship with their advisor and committee in which members worked well together. Others found their committee members difficult to work with, and a few even felt emotionally abused. Every one of the women described the incredible stress inherent in forging a long-term relationship with a dissertation advisor since that relationship was based on a somewhat unpredictable set of criteria.

THE STORIES

Reflected in the women's stories is the awkward and often uncomfortable line between authority and support in the process of writing a dissertation. The dissertation advisor and committee members are the authority for deciding what should be studied, how it should be studied, how it should be presented in writing, and when it is ready to be submitted for the defense. The student is at the mercy of the committee as she figures out *how* to get to the point where she will be ready to defend. Also, in the process of writing the dissertation and dwelling with the source material or data, the student may uncover elements that the committee did not think about with the original proposal. She may feel stuck with the initial plan, unsure of how to negotiate changes or whether such negotiation is even allowed. When is it okay to disagree with one's chair or committee member? What kind of relationship should one expect? And what are the important factors to consider in selecting committee members—besides making sure they are not mean?

Shopping Around for a Committee

In Chapter 2, we discussed the mystery of the dissertation process. The women in our study made it clear that this mystery was not confined to writing the dissertation itself but also related to how to select a committee. Most of the women said they had no idea of how to pick their dissertation advisor or committee members. Some were told to be sure and select committee members who would get along. But how could they know this? It was clear from the women's stories that it was important to select an advisor who had experience.

But this criterion did not always align with someone who had the required background in the student's research area. And then, there were the personal variables to consider: How would the student's personality mesh with that of the advisor and other committee members?

Gabriella shared her insights about important factors to consider in forming a committee and how difficult it can be to integrate these:

I can emphasize how important it is who you select for your committee. Because you need people that can, that are content experts, and can guide you in that regard but also people who believe in you—believe that you can do it—and will support that part. And there are people out there, unfortunately, who are content experts who have the exact opposite approach. You know, they're gonna find criticism in everything you do. You don't want a person like that (laughs) on your committee, you want to try to avoid them! To the extent that you can select your committee members, you should *carefully* select them. . . . The committee is very important to you because they can, they can not only support you through it, they *are* the content experts, so you can go to them for, you know, guidance on details, methods, on fact checks—a lot of things that can be very helpful.

Gabriella had difficulty finding the right committee members, but she seemed to accept that this was a part of the process:

[I encountered] people who said, "You know, I don't think [your topic is] that interesting, I don't want to do that." So they said no to me, and they should, if they find it not interesting, they should say no. . . . I was lucky I got to choose—the responsibility was on me to find people who were willing to work with me on the topic that I was interested in. . . . One person that I asked, asked me who else was on the committee. And I told this person, and was told that, "I can't work with them." So, I mean there, I'm glad they were forthcoming in that—excluded themselves because they didn't want to work with the other people that were on the committee.

Several women talked about the frustration of not knowing a direct way to solicit a dissertation advisor or committee members. Celeste expressed her feelings at having to spend time looking for someone for her committee instead of focusing on the research:

It would help me if they, someone gave some information and some suggestions. . . . "You could go to so-and-so and see what they're doing." . . . I want to avoid that step and focus on the research itself. I want to work on my paper, not who could I find to help me—it's a whole extra step, and I don't think I should have that step.

Mary tried to instill some humor while describing her experiences of forming a committee, but clearly it was a very stressful and somewhat humiliating process for her:

The major obstacles that I had included forming a committee . . . you had to have a chairperson who was tenured, and there was no way to get a list of who was tenured. You had to go ask people, "Are you tenured? Who else is tenured," creating my own list—no idea! And so the way it was sort of recommended was go first to someone who you think might have interest in your area, they have to be tenured and find your chair first and then your chair would then help you choose other people who would be a good adjunct to your team. So I went to five tenured faculty and asked them to be my chair, and every one of them said no. . . . [For most,] it was their workload. One said they felt that they had no expertise. . . . So five people I asked, and they all said no.

So then I went back [to one of the people I'd asked] . . . I went back to her, I said, "I need either you to rethink and maybe accept being my chair or tell me who I need to go to because I don't know who else to go to." . . . So she, I think, felt pity, agreed to be my chair, but I found that extremely . . . I just thought it was a disgrace, to be honest with you, that the school. . . . The way I would set it up is, you know how many tenured people you have, you know, how many dissertations they can carry. If it's ten, six, or three, I don't care. When one drops off, you know you have a slot. . . . But they called it "shopping around" with your proposal . . . I was like, that is crazy. . . .

I spent a little bit of time that summer feeling really rejected, and thinking that it was me, and then I realized it wasn't me, it was them. They didn't have the time; they didn't feel that they could pull it off, at all, because of their workloads. So, they all were just so stressed out . . . what I said to the person I went back to—when I went back to her—I said, "Either you take me, or you tell me who will take me, and then I want that person to know that they have to take me. I'm not going to do this anymore, this is ridiculous." So, anyway she did take me.

Whatever the difficulty of finding the right dissertation advisor and the right committee members, the women agreed that it was an essential part of success in the dissertation process. Naomi summed it up this way:

Make sure that you pick people you can work with, that you get along with. It's invaluable! It's probably more important than picking the right topic—you know, reasonable people. Talk to them ahead of time, talk to other students about who is good to work with and who is really bad because the students all know.

The Ideal Advisor Relationship

We asked the women how they would characterize an ideal relationship with an advisor who would chair their dissertation committee. Their responses reflected the complexity of this relationship. Two people, a student and an advisor, with very busy lives and who know very little about each other, are suddenly thrust together, sometimes for years, to bring this huge amorphous project to life. When one stops to consider this unusual relationship, it is probably no wonder that problems occur along the way. From the interviews, it was clear that in the long process of this relationship, the differing personalities and work styles of the student and advisor were often a part of the stress. Alecia's response conveys the complexity of this relationship, with so many variables to consider:

Whew! I think that's such a hard place to be in, period. Because we can call it a team and we're working together but really aren't, because ultimately they sign off on your life. On some level, that's the whole goal of why you go to school, to have that degree, and ultimately, that person has major control over that. I realized in the middle of my dissertation, why so many people are ABD. It's so clear. It would have been so much easier to say forget it. I think the relationship is difficult. Ideally, you'd want to think of that whole mentor-mentee relationship, where the other person really helps make their strengths available to you to help guide the process. But then, I think it's also an individual thing like some people need more guidance, feedback, direct hands-on. Other people work better independently. Some people need real structure, like turn in this by this date, you know, other people don't. . . . you can't always figure out how the styles will meld together.

Alecia goes on to say that even though these personal characteristics are very important, they cannot always be incorporated if the person does not have the research criteria needed:

You get stuck sometimes because you're researching something in a certain area, and this is the resident expert in the area, and your styles kind of go out the window, and it doesn't matter if the styles mesh or meld, they're going to be your advisor. Hopefully, the committee that you choose can be a variety of people, and I think that's why it's good that you do all those other qualifying exams and those things, so it gives you a chance to see how people work. So, I think it's hard. I mean, the ideal is what works for the individual, but that's tough.

Eleanor longed for a more ideal relationship where the nature and timing of communications could be agreed upon up front:

Some pre-arranged rules, where there would be the more high-stakes communication that would occur after the low-key communication, and I'm not sure about the scheduling, if it's the scheduling itself, or just communicating about the process that might be helpful. But certainly discussion about progress and rates of progress, and difficulties. Maybe setting a schedule and having the means to make it a little flexible. . . .

When asked about an ideal advisor-student relationship, Greta had many answers, showing this subject to be one to which she had already given much thought. She noted that it was important to have a relationship with an experienced advisor, who could not only be effective in guiding the student through writing the dissertation, but also in helping to know what kind of support was needed along the way. Such support might include stepping in to help the student handle demands from other committee members:

My chair was experienced with doctoral students. She had over six pre-doctoral students. She knew what life was like as a doctoral student. And when I was having hard times, she'd say to me, "Well, you know, I just talked to such-and-such doctoral student, who is a little bit ahead, and she said that this is real hard." And she mirrored that, you know, "Greta, I know this is real hard for you right now." She was a good chair. She smoothed the way for me. She took care of bad behavior. . . . One person on my committee, here we are two weeks before I defended, and she had a whole page of questions. Do you know it took me two weeks non-stop researching to get those answers? But as a good chair she said, "Greta, I want you to do all this research. I want you to summarize it, and I want you to email it to me and her"; so two days before we defended, she took charge of the defense.

A good chair is somebody with high ethical standards, somebody who has good communication techniques. Or even if they don't, they know where their weaknesses are. Like she said, "Greta I'm not your counselor." But she gave me the gift of Phil. She was the one that told me "I want you to use Phil." And so when I called Phil up—he didn't know me from anything—I said "Dr. C___ wanted me to call. She thought you could work with me." Okay. All I had to say was "Dr. C___"—that's all, okay? She made sure and did different things. She worked behind the scenes.

So a good chair is somebody also of high, I think, integrity, and I, I never would have thought of integrity. . . .

I believe there is nothing worse for a doctoral student who's in an area that's not well researched to be paired with somebody who's in their first year working with doctoral students. I believe . . . that faculty member should be mentored. You should kind of like have a co-chair . . . a good chair is somebody that is experienced, but if they're not experienced, that they have an experienced person helping them. I think that would be good. Um, that they know how to write.

Um, what else makes a good chair? Somebody that answers your messages. And defines your parameters. Like for instance— "I'm busy writing a grant. I won't be able to get back to you for a month." And that's fine. I'll be working on other things. Or you know, "This is a busy time for me, so I can maybe answer an email. You need to give me five days." And I never could understand that. But they'd say "I need to carve out a time to read what you've given me, and I've given that to next Thursday." I never understood that as a student, but now as a faculty member I do. You know somebody who's upfront with what they can do and what they can't do.

I think also somebody, in this day of technology, I think making time for the personal dialogue, face to face, because a lot of work can't happen on email. In order to construct an email message, you have to be very finely tuned. But how do you write an email message that says "I'm wondering what to do next" or "I'm wondering if I wrote this very good" . . .

I think a good chair connects people. . . . For instance, "I told them about you, so when you call them they know about you because I've already told them about you." That's a good chair. And a good chair needs to know—a good committee needs to be one that gets along. No fighting. And so a good question that you ask a chair is who do you—could you work with? And I don't know if people know all this kind of stuff—this is the stuff that they don't talk about.

Martha suggested that in order to help students with difficult situations that might arise from differing views by committee members, the dissertation advisor should be a diplomat:

I think the chair should, generally, be a diplomat. That's able to, you know, when you have disagreements about any issues, that person is able to help guide the discussion so you can reach a respectful conclusion. That's very difficult when you have a student who's right in the middle of their dissertation. They can't do, they cannot focus on many different things all at the same time. And the other goal is to remove obstacles, maybe try to deal with them. So they may need somebody that's able to help them deal with it. Somebody, I think, that has strong written and verbal communication skills.

Callie found the dissertation process stimulating and her advisor to be ideal insofar as he was an important part of the excitement she felt in the process:

Having that bouncing around of ideas and sharing and learning and—you know, you're so stimulated, you feel fantastic. That's one of the ideals. I did actually—and it's been a fantastic experience.

Monique saw support and expertise as key to an ideal dissertation advisor and also felt that her relationship with her advisor was close to ideal. She was very grateful as she had many unexpected family problems to deal with along the way:

An ideal? I think [the relationship] should be one that is primarily a supportive one. Support because you haven't gone this far not really knowing or having intelligence about how to write and do certain things. So I think you definitely need the support of your advisor, and certainly that person is an expert. That is probably why you chose them to be part of your committee; your expert is someone you feel is important or relevant to your dissertation. So you certainly look to their expertise and look to learn from them and in around that whole area of their expertise. And also in terms of research process, because this is your first for the most part—your first time doing a major research study—so support to me is extremely key—a nurturing and supportive type relationship is very important to me.

Exactly what I wanted is what I got. [My chair] never failed me, in terms I knew I could count on her for support. Life brought lots of twists and turns for me in the midst of working on my doctorate and writing the dissertation. Many things happened to me that you don't necessarily plan for in terms of your family members and people getting sick, dying, and all of that and just those things happen. . . . And always, I could count on her for being supportive and understanding where I was at and giving me time to get myself together. I never quit, I never quit, but I might've slowed down a bit with everything that just happened. But I never stopped. It was a wonderful relationship.

The Real Advisor Relationship

We asked our participants: *Based on your thoughts of the ideal relationship, how would you describe the real relationship that you had with your advisor?* Their answers revealed the intricacies of dealing with the ideal versus the reality in making this relationship work for both parties. It was clear that building an effective long-term relationship with an advisor did not just happen. It took a great deal of thought, strategic steps, and an innate sensitivity to make the relationship work effectively.

We include some long excerpts from Louise here because they illustrate the vulnerability of the student in the complex relationship with an advisor and how critical it is to find ways to communicate well and understand each other's intent in the process. Louise described how differing expectations of student and advisor regarding submitted drafts can create misunderstandings.

I wanted her to recognize—for example, the first chapter, it was really, really bad, it was the first one, and I knew it wasn't a chapter. For me, it was like, well, I've put all my ideas here. Tell me if this is the kind of thing you want. . . . And she didn't get that. She said, "Oh, it's fine, now you've sorted out all the problems, what's your next one?" And I thought, "Oh, okay, I'm fine." Which wasn't true because that was the chapter that I had to go back at the very end, and it was a *lot* of work because it was just like "Wooooooo! I want to deal with everything here." But that's the one, that's one thing you have to start with. And my second chapter, I thought I had a thesis—I did have a thesis, for this one. I was really, really clear, and I started making sense with what I wanted to do with the whole dissertation. The first one was problematic and everything. And I sent her, same thing, the draft, and she liked the idea very much, she says, "This is great, this is excellent," and I'm thinking "Gah, she's doing that to me again. Telling me it's excellent, and then when I'm finished, it's not good, and I don't get constructive feedback in between." I'm like, I don't want to get compliments, I want to know what's good, what's not, and how do I reach the point of making it better? I can't, it's the first time I'm doing this, I can't do everything.

And then she would, she sent me a really mean, I mean a very sharp email. I had sent her, at the end of the summer, my chapter was not ready. The draft was. But it needed probably another three weeks of clean-up. And I was so, I felt so guilty about being late that I said, "Here's my draft. Tell me what you think." I wrote a long memo at the end of the chapter explaining everything and why it was this and that, and that it *was* a draft. She didn't read [the memo]! And that happened *several times*, where I would send an email, and she wouldn't read it, and then she wrote me back and said, "Louise this is really serious. This is not a chapter. There are so many mistakes."

But she wouldn't read the message, because I *knew* it was not a finished product. It was *not*. But then, later she realized there was a memo at the end of the chapter. I should have put the memo first, I don't know, it was just I didn't want to waste paper, I used the back of the chapter. But then, she didn't apologize. . . . I wished she would say, "Oh, I'm sorry, I didn't read your note." But she wasn't because she was afraid that, as a teacher if you apologize in front of your students, they try to take advantage of it. But I'm *not an undergrad*. So that was my frustration, and it happened several times. . . . She was right, the chapter was not ready, but I had just, I had said that to her at the same time.

In the midst of something as long and stressful as a dissertation, even minor misunderstandings can become hurtful, as suggested by Louise's description of how she was hurt by a comment by her advisor that was probably meant to be helpful:

> I would send a chapter that I had revised . . . and she'd say, "Well, there are still a few things. Did you turn on your spell check? Did you know you can buy a spell check?" Yes, the first six months I did not have the spell check for German. . . . And it was true, but it was just said in such a way . . . and then, she did it again last month when she sent me my corrections after the defense, "Did you use—" and it was not the spell check this time . . . and she says, "Did you use the grammar check?" And I was like "Yes, I did." And I just *hate* when she says something like that.

Because of the nature of her academic discipline, Stella had expected her relationship with her dissertation advisor to be collaborative, not that she would be so alone in the activity, but in hindsight, she realizes that her advisor made the decision purposively:

> I thought my advisor's role was going to be different. I didn't think [the dissertation] was going to be quite so much mine. That was something that came out as we went through the process. I thought oh, I'm actually the one writing all this. I was expecting that it would be much more cooperative. And I think my advisor did that intentionally, kind of pulled back. When I started writing my dissertation full time, she stepped back a little bit . . . and I figured out—well my advisor said, at some point, "This is yours, so I'll give you feedback on things that are unclear, but this is yours." And so I was like, oookaaayyyy (laughs).

Audrey considered herself very fortunate to have a good relationship with her advisor, but her story helps to illustrate that in reality, there probably is no ideal advisor-student relationship. Even though the advisor means to be supportive, and the student wants to be open to new ideas and to criticism, the differing personalities and expectations may create conflicts:

> I knew from having gone through this process with a lot of other people and having actually had a support group outside of my

university—lots of people didn't have the experience that I did. I was extremely lucky. I felt that I was friends with my advisor. I felt I could talk to him about things that weren't exactly related to the dissertation. I knew his wife, I knew his daughter—I had a really good relationship with them.

I think that when I saw a lot of other people who had much different experiences, they had absent advisors, or they had overly harsh advisors, or a multitude of other situations and problems that people had, I realize that, yeah, that relationship did help a lot. . . . The idea of I could go in and I could say, "You know, I'm really stressed out about this project," and he would say "It's okay," while at the same time saying, "You have to do this, you need to do this, I'm not going to say take a holiday for three weeks, you have to do it, but I understand where you're coming from."

At one point he sat me down, and he said, "I know that you desperately want to go on the market, I know that there are jobs that, for personal reasons, you really want—you're not there. I can't let you." He said "I cannot let you send out what you've done, because it will hurt you more than it will help you." And that's tough to hear, that's horrible, but I needed to hear it. And I think that without having had a personal friendship with him, that would have been a lot worse.

Even though Audrey had a good relationship with her advisor, she remembers how difficult it was to handle his demanding standards. Her memory of one such event is still vivid months after completing her dissertation:

The first time that I got my advisor to accept something that I'd done . . . where he'd finally said, "Okay, I'll take this chapter," and it was the middle of winter, and it was December, and it was cold, and it was dark despite the fact that it was four o'clock in the afternoon, and I had to take the bus home. And I remember sitting on the bus and going, "I'm never going to get this finished. It took me six months to get him to actually accept a chapter." If it was going to take me six months to get a chapter accepted every time, then it was just *never* going to happen.

Audrey relied on a peer to help interpret some of her advisor's comments that seemed confusing and hurtful, especially coming from an advisor who was a friend:

> I had another graduate student who had the same advisor as me. And she understood how I think better than anybody because she had the same advisor. So she would—we would always contact each other after we had a meeting with him. Because it made us feel better. So she had some phrase that she used for him, something like "his cautiously optimistic praise." (Laughs) And I would say, "Yes, I'm so glad you're having that experience, too, I thought it was just me!" Because he was notorious that he was very, very supportive, but he was notoriously sparse with any praise that he gave, and once I realized that—we both realized that—it's just him, it's what he's like. It's not that he's not saying that this is good because it's awful, he's not saying it's good because he's very cautious with feedback that he gives. It really did help. And we always would [talk] because quite frequently we left his office upset. And the first thing I would do, I'd pull out the cell phone, and I'd call her, and I'd say, "He said this to me," and she'd say, "Oh, yeah, well, that's the kind of thing he says, he said something similar to me when this happened," and she would do the same, she would call me and say, "I just had a meeting," and I'd say, "Oh well, I had a similar experience with him."

Bubbles had known her advisor and his wife for almost 20 years by the time she started her dissertation; so she needed to find a way to maintain this friendship within the more formal student-advisor relationship. Her self-confidence is evident in the clever and graceful way that she handled criticism from her advisor that could have been hurtful:

> Well, so this is funny because . . . he's definitely mellowed out a little in his older age. You know how men get more estrogen as they—so we kind of tease him about that as he is way more nice than when I first started. But I do think that it's partly a personality thing because he is—very direct. And just doesn't really pull a lot of punches; so for example, the very first talk I was working on that I was going to give the department because we had to do this once

a year as a graduate student, give a talk and tell everybody what you're doing—and I'm going through it, you know, and at the end, he's like, okay, well, that was terrible in this slide, oh, that was horrible, what are you thinking—and just kind of this long thing. And I waited 'til he was done, and I said, "Was there anything that you liked about it?" Because he thinks he's helping, you know, and for me, that was fine because if I know that somebody's heart is in the right place, which I *know* that it was based on all of his other behavior and all the times he helped us out by getting us summer support and all kinds of things—I mean that demonstrated to me that "You want what's best for me. Now, your tact level is quite low." (Laughs) Which I have talked to him about since then! But for me, personally, I have a pretty thick skin when it comes to that; so all I can say is I'd rather have somebody say that than say, "Oh, it's great!" and then you go in and make a fool of yourself. So I felt like for me it worked. . . . Those kinds of things to me way outweigh those times when there's not as much polish on things as there could have been, and I would deal with it by just kind of laughing or making a joke of it, and that seemed to work for that sort of situation. So maybe, we're both very flawed people, but together it worked very well. (Laughs)

Gretchen felt that it would be ideal to have a mentor but had to think about whether she did have a mentor for her dissertation. Although her advisor was not the ideal mentor that she might have wanted, she was comfortable with the way their relationship had evolved:

Researcher: Did you have a mentor through the process?
Gretchen: Actually, let me think about this. I didn't really have a mentor I don't think through that process . . . did I? . . . No.
Researcher: Was your chair helpful?
Gretchen: He was responsible and responsive. And I let him know I wanted to graduate in May. And he said, this is what you'll have to do, and we'll do it together. And he's very, kinda hang-loose, qualitative researcher. . . . I was a little concerned that we were gonna get this done. . . . But once he knew that this was our deadline, and I—He

did it! I mean, now I would get, I got my drafts back almost immediately, which is different from some other experiences that I've heard about. So I was grateful for that, too. . . . I remember an email he sent to everybody, and he didn't have to do it more than once. He said, "Okay, here we go, this is what we're gonna have to do!" . . . Very encouraging, and so I had a good experience. I didn't have a nightmare committee experience. Some people do, but I didn't.

Eleanor gradually found a way to work with her advisor effectively, but she needed guidance from fellow students to help her understand his communication style:

I emailed something that didn't involve a direct question, just saying I wanted to make sure this was the correct email address because my work schedule has eased up, and I'll be hopefully sending some things along. Since there wasn't a direct question, I didn't receive a reply. I was told by a colleague who also worked with the very same advisor that that's his style. Unless I were to ask a direct question, he wouldn't be replying back, unless I were to send something, he certainly wouldn't email me to see how things are going.

Many of the women we interviewed were writing their dissertations at a distance from their advisor, and this created additional difficulties in understanding each other. Louise described the difficulty of communicating through email:

It makes it harder because you, you have the message sitting on your desk for a few days. And if you're actually hurt or you're a little angry, and you're just like, "Gosh," you know you don't want to respond that day. You have to wait for like two or three days, and then you read it again, you sort out what actually is not very nice, and then the rest you can see, and then you write an email that's a little sharp—I wrote a couple emails that were very sharp, and she probably thought that I wasn't happy, and she was a lot nicer. But I wish I didn't have to do that.

Claire found that the long-distance relationship with her advisor exacerbated her anxieties about communicating with him:

Sometimes, after we'd had an awkward exchange, then I would just dread getting the next email from him. It was really unhealthy. I'd see I had an email from him, then I'd panic for about a day before I could make myself read it. Most of the time, it turned out I was worrying for nothing. And I knew that. But once in a while his emails would be really hurtful, so I always feared the worst, even though I knew I was just hurting myself with that kind of anxiety.

Several women talked about ways that they found to work effectively within the complexity of their relationships with their advisors and committees. Alecia described how, in spite of not having an ideal relationship with her advisor, she appreciated the complexity of the relationship and valued it highly:

My advisor has been very mentor-like, and even now, it's continued beyond . . . with changing jobs and through everything, she's been really good. . . . I guess any relationship has some rocky kinds of things, and so there was a fair share. She's made up for so much stuff in the time since I've been done, it's harder for me to still hold on to that. At one point, I was furious with her. I thought I'll never talk to her in life, you know, and that hasn't been the case at all. She's continued as a strong mentor, and I hope that relationship continues and continues and continues because it's really beneficial for me.

Joanne figured out how to work with her various committee members in different ways to meet her needs:

I used the faculty advisors in different ways. You know, I had a main person who I would touch base with and share ideas with and back-and-forth and dialogue much more so. Others, I just only engaged when I absolutely needed a piece of information in order to take the dissertation to the next step. I always built in extra time for this one faculty who I knew wasn't going to turn things around within the timeframe that I was asking.

Martha creatively found a mentor who was different from her advisor and used that person to fill in the gaps of what she felt was missing from the relationship with her advisor:

A mentor, I think, is probably different from your committee chair. Now, I had a committee chair that really didn't know much and wasn't really that interested in [my topic]. . . . She was more interested in the process . . . that I demonstrate the process of dissertation work. But . . . I had a mentor at that time who was tremendously interested in this. And so, had I not had the right mentor to, you know, to encourage me and help me answer questions and to deal with issues about [my topic], then I may have approached, not only this dissertation, but my work very differently. But I think as people prepare, you know, will prepare for their dissertations, they need to really think about that. That they may want to have a committee chair that can help them with the mechanics of the process, but if they really want to do something with it, they need to have a strong mentor, that may or may not be a part of their committee.

Your mentor, I see as the person that's gonna challenge you intellectually, inspire the way that you think, and then be somebody that is not only an inspiration but is truly a very in-depth subject matter expert on whatever area you're working in. I think, sometimes, if they're a part of your committee, it sometimes, I think it can be, it can be problematic. Because committees fall out in so many different ways. Sometimes you can get that little bit of conflict between the mentor and, you know, the committee chair.

Best Practices from the Dissertation Advisor

While our women participants were fully aware of the complexity of the long and sometimes arduous process of working with their dissertation advisor, they also noted some best practices of their advisors that were especially helpful to them. When asked "What made the difference for you to be able to persist in writing the dissertation?" Monique responded:

First of all, [my chair] was pretty flexible in terms of meeting. When I finally got to the point where I felt like I needed to, on a daily basis, to be doing something with the dissertation or at least, weekly, with the dissertation, she consented to meet with me weekly because as I was writing, I wanted her to look at what I was writing and see if I was moving in the right direction. "What do you think about this?" Because I wanted to be sure it was a cohesive document moving in the right direction. So she met with me weekly. She met with me at her home. And we met at the restaurant between her house and my house, and we did do that a couple of times as well; several times actually. She was always there—available and flexible. I needed that. I needed that. I mean, that really stands out in my mind . . . just because I wanted to make sure I was making some progress. That just stands out because that was important and I needed that.

For Louise, her advisor's skill in helping her with the writing and organization of her dissertation was invaluable:

I would expect her to put my dissertation in order for me. Which she would do an amazing job, but sometimes, like she would say it was good, but then I knew it wasn't good, and I wanted her to fix everything. But half-way through the dissertation, when I would send a chapter, she said "There's a structure problem here." And I'd be like, "Oh my God, it's terrible." And she's like, "No, you're making these four points here in the introduction, I'd like you to start with D C A B instead of A B C D." And she said, "It just makes the argument much stronger." And that was good because she could read, process, and just say, "I would put that—." And then it's true there wasn't much to do—all I had to do was just cut and paste, add a couple of sentences to reinforce, and that was it.

Callie talked about how important it was for her advisor to help her articulate her thoughts so that she could find the meaning in what she wanted to say:

I think the vibrancy of this professor . . . this is a good example, because this happened last Friday for me, where I'd written down some ideas in terms of the theoretical lens I'm using, I want to use. And it was a fantastic meeting because we're sparking, you know, we're talking. And she's so into the data with me . . . We've got this kind of intellectual tennis game going on, so you're batting it back, and it was just fantastic. I come out with loads of new information and feel proud, you know, of lots of points that I've put forward that she thinks are good. Because she's brilliant, you know, and if she thinks they're good, I know they're good. . . . Lots of people tell you you're doing a great job, and you say, "No, you don't know. You don't know, do you, that I'm doing a great job." But if *she's* telling me that I'm doing a great job, then yes!

In a similar way, Gretchen talked about how her advisor gave her subtle guidance in how to think more deeply about her work:

[She] was fond of using the phrase, "What's going on here?" . . . and so I'd go back to that in my head and ask it, over and over again, "What's going on, what's the story here?"

Mary talked about how she needed her advisor to help her realize that the timeline she had set for herself was unrealistic:

I originally wanted to finish in August, and then I showed [my advisor] my work plan and she said, "You underestimated the back end, after the data was in." I had the data being analyzed in June, and it took 'til August, and then I had revising chapter four, presentation of the data, and then chapter five, interpretation of the findings . . . I was going to finish all of that . . . I was going to analyze my data in June, write all of that in July, and defend in August. She said "You're not going to be able to write that in July." She said, "Are you taking off the summer?" I said no. She said "You're not going to be able to write that because it's not that it's 50 pages that I don't think you can write, it's the synthesis of your whole thing." And she was right about that, it took a lot longer than that.

Several women talked about their reliance on their advisors to help them learn how to negotiate their relationship with others whom they needed to work with. Kim described how her advisor helped in this way:

> When you are going through the process for the very first time, you—I was very fortunate to have my chair of my committee very available even though she said this was a new area for her . . . she would try on her own to find, to answer my questions, or to direct me to a person who might in fact help me. So, when, for example, when my statistics had to be reviewed, both at [my work setting] and at [my university], she made sure that the statistician was of the caliber that she thought was necessary. And it turned out that he was pretty good! Above average! (Laughs) . . . One of the things that she taught me was that you have to negotiate with the people that are connected, your second and third readers, and it was always best to set up a time and then have a fallback, you know: "I would like you to review or read this by, or in three weeks, is that reasonable?" If they said yes, and then the three weeks came and there was no return, then she advised me of what to do next, how to get them—so that they didn't derail my progress.

Never Knowing on Which Foot to Dance

Although the women described many practices by their advisor and committee members that were helpful, they also described how a lack of direction was often one of the most frustrating aspects of the dissertation process. As noted in Chapter 2, the dissertation often unfolded for these women in a confusing set of steps that were difficult to predict or navigate. They wondered why they were not told early on in the process what they could and could not do. They wanted clear directions from their dissertation advisor and committee about what parameters were acceptable. Louise shared her frustrations with this lack of clear and consistent communication: "I never knew on which foot to dance. . . . [The committee] kept changing their minds all the time."

Stella wanted to make the dissertation her own and do it independently, yet she needed more guidance from her advisor in how to do it:

My advisor was not the most socially adept person, but she was the kind of person who, if you ask her something that she would consider inappropriate, she would just tell you, "Oh, I'm not going to answer that." Kind of with, I mean, at some point I would ask her, "Well what do you think I should do here?" She said "Well this doesn't really work," and I'd say, "Well what do you think I should do there," and she'd say, "I'm not going to answer that." (Laughs) Okay! At some point I was really stressed out, and I left her office, and I just went back to my office that I shared with a friend of mine, and I said, "I need you to not talk to me for the next 10 minutes because if you say anything to me I'm going to lose it; so could you just not talk to me for the next 10 minutes?" And so I put on my headphones, and . . . I felt totally abandoned. And the next week, she was much more available to me than she had been for a while; so I think she picked up on that, and in fact, when I left her office, I was on the verge of tears. I joked about that afterwards—apparently she knows when she's pushed you too far. But I never went to her in tears. I always thought, I'll be tough and figure stuff out. But she wanted to be a very good advisor. But I wouldn't say that I felt comfortable being vulnerable around her. And she's not like a warm fuzzy kind of person, she's not the, "Oh sweetie, come here and cry on my shoulder," type. She's much more of the (cheery voice), "Well buck up, you can do this!"

Upon further reflection, Stella wondered whether her advisor's dismissive behavior might have been a strategy to have her work more independently on the dissertation and not be dependent on her advisor:

I think I had become very dependent on her input and guidance, and so she was, I'd find her saying, "Well, I can't meet with you until Friday, so you just have to figure things out until Friday." I think that was deliberate. I didn't know that at the time. At the time, I was very frustrated. But I do think that that was, it wouldn't surprise me if that was a deliberate thing. . . . I think I feel a lot more ownership of my dissertation than I would have. Which I think is good and important.

Celeste articulated her confusion that resulted from the lack of adequate guidance that caused a long delay in her progress:

> If someone is motivated enough to undertake this process, then the other end, on the other end, they should be prepared to help you do this in a clear and concise manner and format so that there is not this level of frustration. And it's not too much to ask. It isn't . . . I was confused and I think other people were as well—I had originally thought that I would do a historical study because there's never been anything done about [that]. So my first proposal was that. And I had gone to [a meeting] with the archivist, I'd already gone through the details to write that proposal, and then they said, no, it has to be quantitative or qualitative. So—not historical. You have to actually do a study versus historical only. So I was frustrated to start with because I'd done a good bit of work on that before.

Still in the process of writing her dissertation, Celeste was so frustrated that she was almost ready to quit and try another institution:

> The backtracking is frustrating. It's time to be moving forward and finishing. . . . It has gotten to the point where I've just thought, well, I'm going to go somewhere else . . . go somewhere else and finish it so that I can, maybe, find this one-on-one or find more what I'm looking for. But I'm not sure it's anywhere. I'm not sure the process is solidified enough or is—that it would help anything. And I'm just so far now—after having done all the classes and the comps and it's just—it's an investment . . . I realize that there are some schools, you pay your money, you write whatever; but you know, here you try and go to a prestigious school where your degree actually means something, and then you reach this point. . . .

Greta talked about how frustrated she was with the lack of guidance for her writing. She would submit what she thought was good writing, only to be told it was inferior. That kind of feedback did not help her understand what was considered "adequate."

You go in thinking you gave it your best work, I mean you didn't intend to give 'em—I mean who intends to give "shitty"? And then people were just like "This is not adequate." . . .

Too Many Cooks

As we listened to the women talk of their experiences with dissertation committees, it was clear that the workings of a good committee are a fine-tuned process. There seemed to be many variables that could affect whether a committee functioned well or not. The personality, work schedule, timeline, academic specialty, research methodology, or writing style of the student, chair, or committee member were only a few characteristics that had to mesh to make the committee work together smoothly. Celeste talked about the difficulty of having too many people advising her, sometimes in contradictory ways:

> *Celeste:* Even in the working, now, they're making other suggestions. Why don't you broaden this to so-and-so, narrow this to so-and-so, so even after the proposal is done, as I'm writing, there are still suggestions coming.
> *Researcher:* And they're coming from multiple people?
> *Celeste:* Yes, from the committee, not from one advisor. And I think that is very detrimental to the process. However many people you have is however many ideas that you have. . . . There's a lot of jumping in by different people so that you're not alone, and with all these folks as your sole responsibility, there's people that are helping and as they say, too many cooks in a kitchen.

Celeste, at times, felt that the "too many cooks" problem was almost part of the whole dissertation ritual, a test from her committee:

You have to *take* it all! And if we tell you to go back, you have to go back with a smile on your face and start over again.

Greta described similar feelings as Celeste in terms of the differing perspectives of committee members:

You're enlisted with all these committee members, and one person's telling you what to do, the other person's telling you what to do, and you're just lost.

Claire was grateful that her advisor stepped in when she encountered the "too many cooks" problem:

I had one committee member who, pretty late in the process, decided she just didn't buy my whole premise as far as I could tell. She didn't like the way I was interpreting the texts I was working with. And another committee member thought my approach was wrong, paying too much attention to the style of the texts I was studying instead of just the content. And I think my advisor somehow conveyed to them, "Look, this is what she's doing. This is what we're going with." So I only had to battle it out with the others a little bit before [my advisor] stepped in.

Keeping Safe and Dealing with Frustrating Committee Members

The women's stories revealed the extreme vulnerability of the students in having to respond to differing perspectives by different committee members and how they needed their dissertation advisor to guide them. Martha saw her advisor as someone to guide her safely throughout the dissertation:

The last thing you want to do is get to your defense and then have a disagreement regarding your methodology or your design or your conclusions or whatever. You need a strong committee chair that can help make, again focus on the mechanics. Make sure that you understand research methodology, that you selected the right methodology for your project, that your project has been designed well. That your written skills are good.

Greta's chair had subtle ways of keeping her safe from hurt:

I tell people the secret to getting through your dissertation: You have a good chair. You have a good fit. . . . There are people that unknowingly sabotage you. I don't think they have any clue sometimes how fragile that doctoral student is . . . and in fact, it's really interesting, [my chair] used to use a pencil—I loved it! You know how some teachers use bright red pen? She used pencil. I love it. . . . She wrote everything in pencil . . . it didn't hurt.

Mary talked about how grateful she was to her chair for saving her from the embarrassment of a wrong statistical analysis:

I did get shaken pretty much when my data analysis was incorrect. . . . The chair asked, "Isn't it yes or no? How can it be overlapping?" . . . I got shaken because I was like, how could I have missed this first and how could these other esteemed people miss this, and then, I was like, gosh, what if other stuff got missed. And so, I really went through again, and I did get a statistician to look again, just at my analysis piece, and I thought, I really hope I'm not putting out something that people are going to pick up and look at and go, what did she do, this isn't even close; she didn't use the right statistical methods. So that kind of, from an intellectual perspective, I was like, I had a few moments where I thought, maybe, I'm not quite smart enough to be doing this, 'cause I didn't even hook up the right stuff, but neither did a PhD in multivariate statistics. So I thought, maybe it's hard, and maybe he missed it, I missed it, we missed it, maybe a lot of people missed it, and wasn't it just good graciousness that we caught it in time, 'cause it could have easily gotten through.

Naomi found one of her committee members so frustrating that she sometimes did not trust herself to respond appropriately without the guidance of her chair. She said:

I often had to, quite often, had to run my responses past my chair or past my husband to make sure that all of the "snot factor" was taken out. Because it really was a very frustrating experience, and

I know that my attitude, I was afraid that my attitude was coming through in my communications with him. And so it took every ounce of maturity that I had to respond professionally.

Sometimes, the chair was not as hands-on, and the student had to find her own way to handle a difficult committee member. Alecia described this type of situation:

One of the people on my committee who was very known in that area, was on the committee, and in retrospect, I would have been better off not even bothering with that, for multiple reasons. On one level, I think he had a real disdain, was not respectful of my field, like I was doing Mickey Mouse stuff, and I went to a top school, a top university and a top school [for my field]. . . . So that wasn't an ideal. . . . He did some things, like I didn't want to use an instrument that his buddy had developed . . . I don't believe in it, and I ended up winning out, and I used the instrument I wanted to use, but it just ended up being a headache, and it was the whole thing like I was having to get his approval. It was like making sure that he was so-called *invested*.

Naomi likewise did not find that her chair supported her when one of her committee members insisted that she analyze her data a specific way, but she finally realized that the committee member was not going to change his mind, and she needed to do it his way:

He wasn't going to change. He wasn't going to back down. That's what he wanted me to do, the data analysis *his* way. He thought he was right. And so I had two choices: I could either quit and give up two and a half years of work, or I could just *do it*! And so I just did it! So I don't know how encouraging that is to other women, but I do sort of tell my students that now. That it's okay to question something the committee says or asks of them. But if they continue to come back and say I have to do this, then just do it! I mean, no matter how unpleasant it is, just do it.

Some of the women talked about their frustrations with the ineffectiveness of their dissertation advisors or how they even felt betrayed by them. Naomi described a difficult situation with her committee in which her chair did not support her in the way that she had anticipated:

> One of the members of my committee, who, for political reasons, was on my committee, but I really wasn't fond of the man . . . he didn't understand my topic *at all*—he was an obstacle. Acted as though he was incensed, distant. Then, it's my understanding from committee work is that the chair can kinda trump everybody else. And so if the chair says, "You're gonna do this," and, you agree to that, then, that's the way it goes . . . but if a reader on your committee doesn't agree, then they take it up with the chair, but the chair always sort of defends you. But that's not at all how it worked for me. . . . I had to do a multiple regression. My chair would not give me any assistance on how to do it. She said, "Do what you think is right." So I did it the way I thought it was correct, submitted it to her, and she was like, "Nah, I don't like that, do it again." And I did that *eight times*! And then she finally said, "Okay, I agree with this. This is correct. We're gonna send it to the readers." So we sent it to the readers . . . and then this man on my committee didn't agree at all. He felt like he wanted me to do it a whole *other way*! So I called my chair, and she basically said that you'll have to do what he told you to do. But she wouldn't defend me, wouldn't stick up, even for her *own opinion*, which was the last way that I did it. So it was very frustrating. . . . It seemed like I spent *hours* writing explanations for things and answering questions that really didn't make . . . it was just a very frustrating experience—it was a real obstacle.

Several of the women talked about how they coped with the frustrations of obstructive committee members, but Audrey's approach was no doubt the most dramatic. It was not until the end of her interview that she shared this story, perhaps because she was more comfortable by then, perhaps because she just wanted to be sure not to end the interview without sharing it, knowing others could relate:

> *Researcher:* I want to make sure I give you a chance to share anything else you'd like to share. Anything that stands out to you . . . (long pause)

Audrey: I think what stands out are the horrible moments that come back to me when I think about it.
Researcher: What was the most horrible moment?
Audrey: (Laughs) One of the moments that stands out to me about my dissertation—the copy of my dissertation that my fourth person had marked up, and it was terrible, and it was absolutely covered in blue pen. I'm pretty sure it was covered in blue pen because about half-way through, I stopped reading. I took it out to the shooting range, and I shot it. I just shot it. I still have it. It's got bullet holes.
Researcher: At what point in the process did you do that?
Audrey: It was about a month after the defense that wasn't, [the defense that got cancelled]. And I was so stressed out, and I was *so* upset with what had happened, I just took it out and . . . I was dating this guy at the time whose dad was a marine, and he said, "Do you want to shoot?" And he asked me "Do you have any interesting things to shoot?" I pegged the dissertation up on the target. I thought it would make me feel better and it did. It really did. And to this day I have that copy of it. I keep meaning to frame it (laughs).

Confidence and Caring

As we listened to the stories of these talented women from diverse disciplines, who had already accomplished so much in their careers, it was poignant to hear how important it was that their advisor and committee members have confidence in them and a caring attitude. The women had friends, parents, spouses, children, and work supervisors who encouraged and believed in them, but in the end, it was the dissertation advisor and committee members—the authority figures—that the women needed to know believed in their chances of success. Bubbles described how important it was for her to do her dissertation in a place where she was respected and where she could do her best work:

I always just felt like everybody's door is open, and I felt like I could just go to somebody at any time and say, "I'm trying to do this, and I don't know how, I'm stuck"—you know, with statistics or something, and that everybody just treated me like a colleague. You know what I mean? I was a colleague, and that's just a great feeling, that you know they respect you, you respect them—I don't know how it happened that way, but it did just sort of pull us into a base that was really fertile for—and I still have great relationships with the professors in my department and try to see them when I can, and they are really just thrilled that everything has worked out like it has, and so I think that a lot of it was just having a place where you can reach your potential. If you're not, if you're just working against the tide all the time, you're going to run out of energy. If you feel like you're working, and others are working with you, then you can get a lot higher. So I do feel like that's how it was—not that everything was perfect or always hunky dory, but for the most part it really was a place where they were supportive and knew that their job was to be a mentor, not my boss or my—you know, you're training me to do what *you* do. And so it just was a great atmosphere.

Louise talked about how important it was that her advisor believed that she would finish her dissertation:

My advisor never doubted I would do it. And she would send me very nice messages once in a while, "You're going to be done," or she would really praise the job when I had just sent her something. And I would *know* when I would get the corrections back two or three weeks—every time I finished a chapter, I got a congratulation message from her, which was *really* nice, "Congratulations, you've done one, this is great." I mean, sometimes it said, "Well, you've done one," or "Let's go to the next one." *But* she always validated that piece of work, even if later she said, "Yeah, this one needs work." . . . But she did that, and when I—she wouldn't hear from me, she would ask me how things were going, 'cause we would communicate by email mostly, and I would ask her if I could also call her for little mini-conferences, telephone conferences where I would say, "Well, this is what I have read, I don't know what to do with this," and the thing is she was always positive.

Advisor and Committee

When asked what she would have expected from her advisor or committee in terms of support that she didn't get, Louise said:

I wanted them to be a little warmer . . . that it wasn't all black and white. There were times where I would get very nice messages—every time she left the country or went to travel, she would tell me, "I'm going to be gone if you send something," or I would get that automated message from the email saying she's out of the office. And, yeah, I wanted—but I think she also realized that herself because there were times she was very warm, and she talked to me like I was an adult, and there were other times I felt *patronized*. And then other times she would be *harsh*, and maybe three times I did cry . . . but I also realized it was the stress, and, but then I would reread the message, and I'd be like, "That's not right, why is she telling me this?" And then later it would be like, "She was right, but she could have said it in a different way." The way she phrased things, it was like "There's a big problem about this." And I hear "big problem" thinking *major* problem. And then I talk back with her, and she says, "No, I didn't mean it that way, Louise, I'm just thinking about a few hours of work."

This was somebody I really admired. I took a couple of classes with her, and she was always somebody I would ask for help once in a while, and then I would talk about what I wanted to do . . . I *really* trusted her. And I felt like I learned so much. And I always felt like she was so nice to me and sweet, that it was just the right person for me to work with. And I don't know if—I think she was afraid of me wanting to—being too close to her, which, I wouldn't call her every day, I never would have called her even every week. I wouldn't have said, "Let's go watch a movie," you know, I wouldn't have done that. But I expected maybe, 'cause when I would drive nine hours to go see her twice a year. . . . the first two years I did that. I would go for five days to a week and stay with friends and work in the library so I could see her a couple times during that week. That was for me very important, just to go there and just keep in touch and be physically there. But I would be disappointed 'cause then I would go, the first time she was so excited to see me, we went out for lunch, and maybe I was too personal, I don't know, then later we wouldn't have lunch, and I'm like, "I drove nine hours!" I'd like to go out for lunch, you know, and talk for an hour, and even if everything won't make sense, that would be nice. I didn't know what to do with my information, but I wanted somebody who would be there when—give me an hour of her time once in a while. . . . So I wanted that, and once we met at the cafeteria at school, and it was a *half hour*, and I said "Well, I don't know exactly what I want to do," and she said "Well, what did you read?" and I tried to sort it out, and she says "Well, I think you're fine. Go work." And I felt like—I did feel a little patronized."

Louise was able to see that through the years, she herself had changed, and it took her chair awhile to realize this change in her:

I think in terms of being patronizing, I think she must have realized that, because toward the end I had to call a few times about administration papers, and one day she said, "Oh, are you staying in town a little longer, I wanted to see you more," and I said, "No, I can't, I have to go home, and we have to take care of the dog." And she said, "Oh, I forget you have responsibilities now." And she told me this, and in a nice voice—and I'm thinking—I didn't want to say, "Yeah, I *do*." That I'm 33, I do have a house, I do have a dog, I have a full-time job, but she would say, "I forget that." I think she still saw me sometimes the same way I was when I arrived in grad school, when I was 25, and I was like, "No, I'm not like this."

Claire confessed that she recognized some of the care she got from her advisor only after she had completed her PhD:

At the time, I just knew he wasn't giving me what I needed. His feedback was harsh, he wasn't willing to help me in early stages of chapters, and he wouldn't even give me advice on how to handle my committee during the defense! He even made some alarming comment the day before my defense that he wondered about my ability to teach as an expert in my field at a research university. And I thought, is this guy going to tank my career just when I'm starting? Does he really think that little of me? Seriously, I went into my defense wondering if it was all for nothing because my own advisor was going to stop me from the career I wanted. But, in fact, I defended successfully, and then I got my dream job first try on the market, so he must have written me a good recommendation. And I realize now that he probably stuck up for me during my dissertation process when I had to petition the university for more time to complete it. So it's like, he was looking out for me along the way, but not in ways I could see at the time.

Mary talked about how she appreciated the personal interest that her chair showed in her and her caring approach:

She's just so caring that when I really had that crisis at the end, she called me at home that night, and she talked me down, and I felt badly, because I knew how busy she was and everything else, but I really needed her to talk me through it, 'cause I'm like, now you've been through 250 of these. I've never been through any. But she lent perspective . . . and she had enough experience to say, "You're going to be fine, you can finish this in two weeks, you're going to be able to do it," and you get through it. So those are the pieces that she offered, and at the end, I was like, "I know you didn't really wanna be the chair of my committee, and I know you said no in the beginning, but I'm so grateful that you said yes." And I think she, I do think she enjoyed it . . . she is great.

Reflections on the Stories

As mentioned at the beginning of this chapter, no topic was brought up more often by the women in our study than their struggles with their committees. From the initial procedure of selecting the dissertation advisor and committee members, through the long process of writing the dissertation and the final steps in preparing for the defense, the vulnerability of the women was apparent.

In listening to their narratives, we heard far fewer stories about the content of the dissertation itself than about the process. They talked about frustrations, resentments, and joys that they experienced in the process of trying to forge effective relationships with all those whom they needed to satisfy in order to complete the dissertation. Even though the content of each dissertation was discipline-specific, and thus they were widely varied, this variation was not evident in the women's descriptions of the process. Whether the research involved collecting scientific data for statistical analysis or reviewing ancient texts in order to articulate a new understanding of the literature, that aspect of the dissertation process did not seem as significantly problematic to the women we interviewed. It was the intricate process of negotiating their relationships with the committee that was most prominent in their memories.

Given the complexity of the committee-student relationship for the student, perhaps it should not be surprising that these women had such vivid memories of the highs and lows of the relationship. As reflected in previous chapters, in the process of writing a dissertation, the student realigns relationships with family members, friends, and co-workers and may realize profound changes in her own self. In addition to all of these changes, the student must integrate herself and her life goals into the small space that is controlled by a group of relative strangers—her dissertation advisor and committee members.

Listen to Claire again as she looks back on the relationship with her advisor that at the time of writing her dissertation felt so adversarial: "So it's like, he was looking out for me along the way, but not in ways I could see at the time." The women in this study clearly experienced narratives of continuing development as they forged new relationships with their dissertation advisors and committee members. It is uplifting to think that as these women found their way through the unknown landscape to complete the dissertation, they grew through their own periods of knowing and unknowing. But what do we know of the growth of the dissertation advisor and committee members in this process?

It seems likely that most, or nearly all, advisors and committee members do want the best for their students but do not necessarily foresee the problems they might cause with a particular kind of criticism or a certain style of communicating and relating. The philosopher Hannah Arendt discusses the unique frailty and unpredictability of human interaction: "The smallest act in the most limited circumstances bears the seed of . . . boundlessness and unpredictability; one deed, one gesture, one word may suffice to change every constellation. In acting . . . it is indeed true that we can really never know what we are doing."[1] A delay in feedback, a helpful suggestion that seems patronizing, a choice not to help because the student needs to be on her own at this point—any of these actions might seem to change "every constellation" for the dissertator in ways the advisor might never predict. But Arendt's philosophy does not suggest that such unpredictability lets us humans off the hook. On the contrary, "though we don't know what we are doing when we are acting, we have no possibility ever to undo what we have done. Action processes are not only unpredictable, they are also irreversible."[2]

What can advisors, committee members, and the students themselves do, then, in the face of such irreversibility and unpredictability of human interaction? Arendt suggests:

> The possible redemption from the predicament of irreversibility is the faculty of forgiving, and the remedy for unpredictability is contained in the faculty to make and keep promises. The two remedies belong together: forgiving relates to the past and serves to undo its deeds, while binding oneself through promises serves to set up in the ocean of future uncertainty islands of security.[3]

We can forgive, and we can make and keep promises. That is what all parties in the dissertation process can do to help themselves work together and understand each other. A student does not help herself by staying mad at her advisor, especially if the hurt was unintended; forgiveness is the best way to return herself to a path to move forward with the dissertation. And advisor, committee, and student would do well to make promises to each other—about process, about expected outcomes, about timelines—and make every effort to keep those promises.

Readers who are approaching the challenge of selecting a dissertation committee may want to ask themselves and others: What things should I look for when asking faculty to be on my committee? How do I go about the process of asking them? What characteristics are important for my ideal advisor? Readers who already have an advisor might want to think about the following questions and then discuss them with their advisor: What is the best way for me to get started on the dissertation? What should the final product look like? What aspects of communication with my advisor are most important to me? Can I send a rough draft of a chapter or should it be polished? What type of feedback is most important to me? What is a reasonable time to expect feedback? Since a great deal of the writing of the dissertation is done in isolation, it is very important to know how to get questions answered along the way. If the student is open with the advisor about what she needs, it is likely to help the advisor as well as herself.

In the process of doing this research, we heard only the voices of students. It would be interesting to hear stories of how dissertation advisors and committee members approach their roles, not just in helping the student with disciplinary research methodologies, but in helping to guide the student safely through that unknown landscape. We encourage students who read this book to seek out conversations with their advisors and committee members in the hope that each can better understand the expectations, limitations, hopes, and needs of the other. And we hope that advisors and committee members who read this book will listen to the voices here that express vulnerability, trust, and need for guidance.

Chapter 6

End of a Journey and a New Beginning

I had a bit of a roadblock in my dissertation where I had a defense cancelled. So when the other two [students] passed, I was looking to the summer to revise and do it afterwards. But another member of the group . . . she had her defense cancelled as well. And it was pretty horrific because we were in this group, and two of us had our defenses cancelled—and I think that gave us something to hold on to because the other lady who had her defense cancelled was really good. And I did a conference with her later, we organized a panel for a conference, and she's just, she's fantastic; I love her work, she's a really competent person. And I thought, "Well, it's not just me. If there's someone who's this competent and had the same thing happen to them, then it's not me, and it's all right. That's okay.

— Audrey

The doctoral defense differs between disciplines, institutions, and countries, but there are some common characteristics. It is usually the last formal step before the dissertation is submitted, and it is often scheduled with an open invitation to the academic community to attend. During the defense, the dissertation advisor usually introduces the student with a little background information, and then the student presents a formal summary of her research. After this summary, the advisor and committee members take turns asking the student specific questions about the research and plans for publication. The questioning may then be opened up to the audience, which may include peers, faculty, and family members. The entire defense may last up to two hours. After the questioning is ended, the student and audience leave the room, and the student paces the hall or seeks comfort from visiting friends and family while the committee discusses the student's work, and votes to pass or fail. In some institutions, the defense represents a final examination where the student may actually fail. For others, it is more of a rite of passage; any serious errors have (hopefully) been pointed out ahead of time and corrected, so that the student and committee can feel fairly confident that the student will have a successful defense.

The Stories

When envisioning the probable content for this book, we did not anticipate including a chapter on the defense. In fact, the defense was not even a subject we planned to bring up in the interviews. As we conducted our early interviews, however, it became clear that the participants wanted to talk about this phase of the dissertation process and that it was a critical aspect for women writing a dissertation—"the coronation," as one of Alecia's committee members referred to it. Although the term "defense" suggests an intimidating process, where the student is challenged to defend the accuracy and quality of her research, we found that for some participants, the defense was a highly anticipated and even welcome part of the dissertation process; they expected that phase to go smoothly and felt well prepared. Others thought they were prepared for the defense but then felt blind-sided by one or more of the committee members during the defense itself.

These women remembered the defense more as a challenge or even nightmare.

The Coronation

Most of the participants felt that they were prepared for the defense by the time they got to that stage and did not really worry about failing, but still their anxiety was intense. Greta's advisor worked with her carefully to help her prepare for her defense:

A week before my defense she gave me eight pages of questions that were the hard questions. . . . And it took me a lot of time, but I answered them very carefully. [My advisor] was very good. She helped me to prepare for every part of the way to anticipate barriers and solve them before they happened to me. So we—I came to my defense with eight pages that I sent to this problematic person [on my committee] before I defended that day that answered every objection that she had. And I was well ready to defend everything.

Gretchen talked about how important it was for her to have her family share in the excitement of the defense with her:

The two older ones [of my children] sat in on my defense. My husband didn't want to. He thought he would jinx it. He thought I would laugh or something (laughing). . . . And so he said "No, I think I'm gonna just wait for you." But I was just so excited and proud to have my two older boys there. They were both in college . . . and they specifically made time to come and do this, to come and support this. And to want to *hear* it. And then they went out. You know the committee said, "Everybody out so we can talk with the candidate." And they went out and said to my husband, "So that's what she's been doing all this time!" (Laughs) And it was *great* because then they understood! They understood exactly what the deal was. And they were extremely proud! And then, let's see, I remember that was, was that a Monday, or Friday? Tuesday? I don't know what day of the week it was, but I *do* know, I defended early enough that we were able to get back on the road and go straight to the soccer game at the high school . . . I was *way* up here (gesturing above head), I was high, and you know that his friends at the soccer stadium turned around and greeted me as Dr. Gretchen! It was fabulous!

It was while preparing for her defense that Stella finally realized her advisor was very helpful and supportive. Her description of the defense is like so many of the women's descriptions of this ritual in that each detail of the "coronation" was important and memorable:

After that really difficult last month, I realized now that my advisor really was supportive! So everybody left the room, and she said, "Well, I've been working with Stella the past five years, and I know all about her stuff, and I really don't have any questions for her. So she stayed and moderated, basically. She didn't answer questions for me, but yeah—the process was the same across our department. You gave a public defense, then you had your private Q and A, then you'd walk out of the room, and you'd be out in the hall, and our department was all one hallway in this gigantic building. And so you'd walk down the hallway and talk to people in the hallway, and then your committee members would come out after a few minutes and say, "Congratulations," and then your advisor would serve champagne. And that was actually the tradition in our department. And so she had a bottle of champagne, and then I had brought a bottle of sparkling apple cider, and actually, my husband was at the defense as well, so that was all really nice.

By the time I got to my defense, I'd had a lot of harder hurdles to overcome, and I knew my committee had all read it and had a chance to give feedback, and I knew my advisor would not let me go up there if I wasn't going to pass. As long as I didn't freak out. As long as I didn't fall apart. As long as I could present my research competently, I was confident I would pass. . . . And I think, if I was at a place that did not foster that feeling, I would not have wanted my family and friends there. Because having them there felt more like a wrapping everything up. And because it had that feeling, it felt really comfortable to have my family there.

During our interview, Gabriella specifically asked if she could talk about her defense because there were aspects of it that she felt were especially important to share:

Okay, there is an interesting event that I think I can interpret. And so, defenses are very stressful because you know that you are sort of on trial, in a certain way, for the work that you've done. I have heard, and many people have stories, of you know, horrible things that happen at defenses where people make them go back and do the whole thing all over when you're, you think you're done! You know when you get there. And so, at a defense, I present the project and answer questions, and then one member of the committee started asking about one particular piece of one chapter, which maybe wasn't as well developed as it could have been. And I said, "You know, well, it is a very important issue, but it is one that could be the subject of a dissertation itself. I mean it's separate, it's a problem area that needs to be developed more. And here's how I propose to think about it in this case. And you know, I guess I could go back and do more, but I'm not sure how much it would add." I really do believe that the chair of the committee supported that, and you know, what I had just said because when I left the room, I think, I mean I didn't hear any of this, but I think he kind of said, "You know, look, you can continue to work on these things for the rest of your life if you want to, but this is, this is good for where we need to be." So they kept it.

Mary described how even though she had a lot of experience in public speaking, the process of the defense was still very frightening, for as she said, the dissertator finds herself in a space where she both is and is not an expert:

One of the faculty had asked if I would come and talk a little bit about getting ready, and somebody was there who had just defended three weeks before, and she made a comment which I agreed with afterwards. At the time, I was like, oh, please . . . and she said, "I have presented to national audiences . . . I've probably given 200 speeches in the last ten years, that's probably a conservative estimate. I'm in front of groups all the time, big groups of three hundred, small groups of ten, medium groups of 50 every week, and have taken platform coaching . . . really done a lot of work to get pretty good at presentation skill sets. I'm not an A, but I'm like a B+ or B–." But this person said she felt like the dissertation defense was completely different from any speech she had ever given. . . . And she said because you're speaking in research language, and you're sharing your research, and people are suddenly asking you questions about your research, and all of a sudden, you're in a space where, it's not that you're not confident, but you're not an expert. You're really a novice in describing research, especially alone. She said it was just so weird. So, for me, you have about 20 minutes to present your work, and then it went over an hour, an hour and maybe 15 minutes of questions, 'cause two hours total . . . of questions, and I had a lot of people come, so it was kind of a free-for-all. And I can remember, at one point, I had done my 20 minutes, and then it was 30 minutes in, 40 minutes in, and I remember I had another hour to go, and I remember looking at my clock, and I don't know if I'm going to be able to continue like this because these people are like chewing away at me. And I hoped to God, as they got deeper and deeper, and deeper into it, I'm like, I'm not going to be able to answer something.

Mary's story illustrates how an experienced and supportive committee can help the student put the defense procedure in perspective so that she can feel more like a colleague than a powerless student:

I had already talked to [committee member] about what if they ask me a question that I don't know the answer to. "Well, darling, the response is 'thank you so much for that insightful question, that sounds like a good topic for some post-doctoral research . . . next question?'" She said, "Look, the only questions that you have to answer are the ones from the three of us, and the rest of these people can leave the room if it gets a little too dicey." So I was like, okay, okay, so I wrote down on a card "post-doctoral research." So, I thought it was very, very rigorous. I thought it was very, very different from anything I had ever done before, so different, and there was no part of that that was a cakewalk for me. If I had just been able to present the stuff and leave, that would have been one thing, but having to answer all those questions, and having people say what about this, what about this, why'd you do this, why'd you do that. But I do think it went in the air of . . . it truly is a scientific presentation of your work . . . so they talk about peer review—these are your new peers, the doctorally-prepared faculty of the school that you think you're going to teach. These are the people you're going to teach with, so if you cannot be at that level of intellectual capacity, it's a pretty big signal.

Kim felt confident going into her defense because of her university's safeguarding of the process leading up to the defense, along with her own experience:

The neat thing about [my university] is when you go to defense, it's not iffy: you have a pretty good idea, they've prepared you enough, so that it's in good enough shape . . . where you have no idea what they're going to ask you, and you have an opportunity to present your problem in a compact way, and then they ask you questions. And so that, in itself, I think is very good, and I was competent there because I've sat on so many IRBs [Institutional Review Boards] and scientific reviews that I knew the hard questions (laughing) that they might ask, and so actually it was very fun for me.

Audrey talked about the public aspect of a defense and how one friend had such a positive impact on her during her defense:

I remember this because she was sitting down at the end of the table to the right—my friend who was a real help, and the reason for this was just before the defense, she looked at me, and she smiled and said, "I'm not going to ask you anything. I'm just here for moral support." And I think because she said that, she became very much a focal point for me because she declared before she went in, "I am here for you, I'm here solely for your moral support, I'm not going to ask you anything, I'm not going to do anything." And that meant so much to me. It really did. Because I felt as if anyone else in there could ask me something, and anything they asked me had the potential to be something I wouldn't know, or I could make a fool of myself, but because she said this I knew she wouldn't do that, and so I was *very* grateful she was there. And I was very grateful that she said that. It was great that she knew to tell me that. Because I didn't know 'til I was standing in the spot that that's what I needed.

The tradition at Bubbles' school was to have a defense that was open to the public, and then another that was a time for the committee to ask questions about the research. She found both of these very enjoyable:

You give an initial presentation that's open to the entire campus. In my case, pretty much it was people from the department and my dad that were there, which almost made me choke up when I was in there, because my dad is so special to me. And seeing him out there, it was really nice. . . . And then, maybe like a week or two later, I had the closed part of the defense, which is you and your committee and your advisor in a room. Our committee had to be five people, your advisor and four other people. And they're supposed to have read it and then ask you questions. Well, it took three hours, but I found it very fun. So to me it was like a fun, we're colleagues, and we're just talking about these things, but I also felt very confident because I think I had five chapters, and they had all already been published except for one. So what are you going to say? I mean it's already gone through peer review and everything.

While not necessarily using the term coronation, many of the women expressed similar sentiments about how they felt once they knew they had passed the defense. They knew they had successfully completed a rite of passage and were now better prepared to go on with their life and career goals. Claire commented that she sensed a changed—and improved—relationship with her committee as soon as she passed her defense:

My advisor came out to tell me I passed, and he shook my hand, and then suddenly everyone on the committee was shaking my hand, some even smiling, congratulating me, treating me almost— almost!—as one of them. I wasn't just a student anymore. For the first time in my life, I wasn't just a student!

Something Happened on the Way to the Coronation . . .

Several of the participants described horror stories they had heard of students having their defense cancelled at the last minute. Greta was shocked at the lack of accommodation afforded her friend:

I had a friend who was supposed to defend her dissertation in two weeks, and I had been all set to go up there for her defense, and she was told that "No." She's finished. And she was dismissed from the program . . . You know I could see as a teacher, myself—this is not representing what we want to have our graduates—but they did not look at the context of where the student was. Her dad was dying. He died without—I think he died during the time that she was writing that. She had awful people on her committee. She was on her fourth chair. And the chair that she had now was an asshole. She was just awful.

One can imagine not only the empathy but the fear that might come from seeing a friend's defense cancelled. Audrey actually had her own defense cancelled. She realized, however, that the situation was not all about her or her own deficiencies, and she came to see it as a growth experience. Her story suggests how the defense is not only difficult for the student but also for the dissertation advisor. Who mentors the novice advisor, who has to make an informed decision about when the student is ready for the defense?

I think my advisor made a mistake. He put through something that wasn't passable. And he was supposed to be the first judge of it. And I think it was embarrassing for him as well because he put something to my committee that he judged as passable, and the rest of my committee read it, and they said we have serious reservations about this. But what they did was they told me—I think maybe it was two days before—they said, "Okay, we have serious reservations about this. We're cancelling your defense." . . . So they made me come in, and my committee told me what I needed to do and what was wrong with it. . . . That was the worst moment of the entire process, was being in that room, and my committee themselves were very reasonable. They were very supportive, they'd all written out notes, which they gave me about what it was that I needed to do, and they spoke to me, and they said, "Well, we know that you're going to pass this." That was fine.

Some of the participants characterized the defense process as "abuse." For Audrey, even though her committee met with her after her first defense was cancelled and tried to prepare her for the rest of the process ahead of her, she found that when the actual defense occurred, she still felt blindsided:

My fourth committee member was on the committee only because he had to be—he was the head of the graduate group—and his work wasn't in my area, it was in a slightly different area, but one that I'd touched on in the course of the dissertation, and for some reason, he thought that it was a good idea to completely humiliate me. And what he did—and it's hard to understand what he did. Because the rest of my committee said, "You need to look at some of your language. Some of the way you phrase things isn't making a great deal of sense, it's not the standard that needs to be used." But this guy had marked the one passage in my dissertation that was the worst paragraph in the 220 pages. One paragraph. And he proceeded to stand up and get the attention of everyone, and say, "This is unacceptable." And he read through the paragraph in a slow and sarcastic voice. Emphasizing every place where the language sounded silly, or I repeated myself, or . . . it was awful. Now my advisor actually—he wouldn't let me go when this was over, he said, "Look, stay there, I'm coming out." And he took me, and we walked around the campus, and he said, "Look, you handled that really well." But I said, "Why did this guy have to ritually humiliate me?" He said, "Just, just don't worry about it. That was very hard to hear, and you stayed and kept your composure." Of course I was dying inside! But apparently, I looked quite composed as he was talking to me, and that was—that was absolutely the worst moment, and I still to this day have no idea why he thought that that was justified.

As Audrey continued with her story, she thought about what she wished she had done differently to gain control of the situation. She also shed light on how the makeup of the dissertation committee can dramatically influence the process of the defense:

I felt afterwards that I should have stopped him. If I'd had the courage to, I would have said, "Fine, I understand what you're saying, can we move on?" But I think my advisor, at that point, was a bit too junior, and this guy was his boss. I think perhaps, my third committee member who used to be the head of the department would have been the one to say that, but she's not the type to really intervene. I didn't feel that—I mean I felt very much that my committee were on my side, and that whatever this guy was doing was . . . unfair . . . so I sort of had the confidence that it didn't really diminish me in the eyes of my committee, who were the ones who were really important, not just that fourth guy who was there because he was the head of the graduate group.

Louise also remembered her defense as traumatic. Her story illustrates how seemingly trivial issues can become huge if the advisor does not manage the process of the defense effectively:

During the defense, one of the jury members didn't like the fact that most of my quotations at the time were all in German. I still had a few to find or translate, I didn't have time, I was going to do that after. They were in German, the primary sources that were in German, but my advisor, even for articles that were in English, throughout the year—that Spring semester—decided that, after reading the last couple of chapters, that I should either translate them or find them if the article had been translated. Well, that's great. So there would be a continuity in the language. I said that's good, but that takes time. Well, when I went to the exam, one of the jury members didn't like that, which is silly because it's just (snaps), it can be changed one way or another, and it's not, it doesn't diminish the value of the work. He didn't want me to translate quotations from English articles, even if what I had done, I would translate in the text and leave a footnote with the original. He said, "No, this was written in English, you leave it in English." And I remember staring at my advisor thinking, "Are you going to say something? Are you going to say something?" She's not.

And she knew—and that's why I'm like, "Hey, that was your job," and she could have said, "Well, I asked her to do this because I thought it would be more consistent." And the [committee member] kept pushing me like, "Why are you doing this? It's stupid."

To make matters worse, Louise felt betrayed by her advisor, who denied that she had given advice to keep key quotations in their original German and, through that denial, left Louise hanging at her defense:

I didn't want to put her in a difficult position, but it was the truth. I said "Dr. ____ asked me to do that, so I guess for consistency." And she said, "No, you probably didn't understand me very well." I am not making this up. I am not exaggerating. So I had a few moments during the defense where I thought, "You—thanks for sticking up for me." I mean it's not much of a deal. I know he's being aggressive, and I don't know if he's just—whatever his deal is, and you don't want to get involved and just let him talk, but this is something you asked me to do, and you could just, "Well I asked her, I thought it would be better, and maybe you're right." You know? She made it about me not understanding her directions. And I was like, "That is not true."

It is clear from Alecia's story of her defense that it was a very painful experience for her, but through time, she has come to realize that the fault was not all hers:

[One committee member] was very difficult in the defense, and instead of just having me rewrite and give them to my chair, his thing was that I needed to come back and defend again because that's like your *coronation* and how could they deprive me of this, and he was the only man, and in fact, at that point, the women sat back and let the man. . . .

In fact, now I talk about this so differently because before, I owned it, and I thought that I had just messed up so horribly, that I had done all of this. And now, I can look back and say, okay, I know I had to do rewrites, and I never expected not to, but I also know that I could have done them and submitted them to my chair and been through, without having to go through that whole extra step. . . .

End of a Journey and a New Beginning 151

I fault [my chair] because she could have spoken up in my defense. Do you know what I mean? And so she didn't do her full responsibility in that one because she should have spoken up . . . "You could have said something or you could have done something," but for me, it still meant that I knew that I was going to walk out of there with this degree, so okay, fine, we'll play this your way. It was interesting, though, because the day of the [second run at] so-called coronation, he was late, he didn't show up. He decided he could bring his wife to the airport that morning, and he got caught, which is crazy because [that city's] traffic is ridiculous, and he got caught in all this traffic, and so he walked in like by the time they were having the party. 'Cause I think they were fed up by then too. . . . And probably, if I had told you this story within maybe six months or three months or so of this happening or within that time, I would have said, I just messed up so horribly. . . . Since then, I realized . . . I've come to say, okay, I really wasn't so awful terrible. . . . So, I've just kind of written him off as a potential person who I don't care if I never see again or have to work with or any of that kind of stuff (laughs).

In summary, good, bad, or ugly, it was clear that the participants saw the defense as a critical signpost in the dissertation process. In spite of the problems that Audrey had with her defense, she was able to reflect on it with humor. Asked about what happened during the defense, the details of what she does and does not remember are interesting:

I think I might have blanked that out. I really can't remember. I remember the shirt that I was wearing! It was my best shirt, it was cornflower blue, and I was wearing a green suit, and I remember because I got a skirt, and the first skirt was too short, and it had to match the color . . . I was looking very professional. I remember that I had a handbag. I don't remember anything that I said. I'm sure I have that in my head somewhere, but it escapes me. I remember that the fourth guy and the third guy ended up in an argument about something. And I tried to intervene because I thought, "This is *my* defense!" (Laughs) . . . And I remember what my third committee member did, was famous for doing. He'd say it was great, it was great, there were no problems, and then he'd throw you a curveball in the defense. And he did. And I was prepared for it, and I didn't even think, what the students who had gone before me thought—what a jerk, why could he not have gotten this out beforehand. But he asked me some really hard question—he asked me what another scholar would have thought of one of my chapters. So he said, "You quoted this scholar, but surely his philosophy on this is blah blah blah blah blah, and what would he think of it?" And I went, "huh?" I don't remember how I answered it. I remember what he asked, but what I said, not a clue.

Claire expressed similar thoughts in recalling her defense, realizing that details of the conversations escaped her very soon after the event:

It was almost like an out-of-body experience, or like someone else was answering the questions. I remember, even during the defense, thinking, "who is saying this stuff?" even though I knew it was me. Especially the more detailed, really expert stuff—maybe I couldn't quite believe I could speak that way! Also I think it was because I was so nervous. And afterwards, I tried to tell friends about an argument I'd gotten stuck on with one committee member, whom I thought was being just willfully difficult, but I couldn't really recapture the details of the argument. It was already gone. I remembered how I felt about it, but not what she and I had said.

Mary's comments illustrate how the distance of time can help to see the defense as a valuable symbol of completion and even "fun":

It was like the bungee jumping of a 45-year-old woman. It's kinda how I felt. It was a huge risk. I just felt like so much was on the line, and I had worked really, really hard, and it all came to that point, and I found it to be really, really intense, and I was completely exhausted when it was over. I was just—but I was so glad I did it, because I don't know what other kind of thing I'd get to do when you're past kind of your growing up milestones that charges you up that much. It was just like, God, I can't believe this. It was unbelievable. So, I'm really very, very happy. I felt like, not only did I pass, but I thought I did a very good job, and I was able to get through some, I thought some pretty challenging stuff. . . . For some people, they have to show how smart they are, so let's attack this poor little doctoral candidate, like, "I'm smarter than my peers." And then, you're like "Yeah, you're smarter than me too, but you don't have to show it right now!" (Laughing) It was something. . . . If you don't know what the questions are, you can only get a good night's sleep and come in with your best foot forward, and you know, look to your committee if you're dying. And my statistician guy did help me on some of them, you know, why'd you do this, and why'd you not do this, and he goes, and before I could even open my mouth, he was like, "I'll take that question," like "huh, who are you?! I'm the one who told her to do this!" (laughing) So, that was fun.

Gabriella also used the word "fun" and described the excitement of ending her defense with the knowledge that someone actually wanted to publish her dissertation:

They did pass me! (Laughs) And that's fun—once it's over, you leave the room, they have their deliberations, and then they call you back in and they say you passed or you didn't. . . . And the way you know you passed is they bring out a bottle of sherry and put it on the table (laughing). And so there's sherry in little cups and everybody has a little drink of sherry. . . . But the fun part of that story for me was once that ritual happened, the person who was the head of [an important initiative] at that point-in-time, came in to join us in the toast. And he said to me, "Would you, would it be okay with you if I got my publisher in touch with you, because I think you need to put this into a book." And I said, "Uh-ah-oh! Sure! (laughing) What the heck! You know, have the publisher call me!" (laughing more) So the guy, the publisher called me a few days later and he, maybe it wasn't a few days, 'cause I had to send it to him, so it must have been a few weeks. But, he called me a little bit later, and he said, "We really like your dissertation, we want to make it into a book." And I just almost fell on the floor, because I said, "Wow, you not only, you not only passed me, but now they want to publish this thing?" (laughing loudly) and he's like, "Yes." And then he went on to talk about royalties. And then you can imagine how I fell off the floor. I said, "You're going to publish it, *and* you're going to pay me for it?" and he said something like, "How many other publishers have you sent it to?" and I just laughed, and I said, "I haven't even turned it into the graduate school yet, of course, I haven't sent it to any publishers, I haven't even thought about that." So that was a kind of fun outcome at the end.

Bubbles expressed her reaction to the defense in terms of relief, as she realized she had passed the final significant step to completing her degree:

I did feel really relieved, and I was ready to be done and ready to move on; as much as I loved that place, I was very ready.

Reflections on the Stories

All of the participants recalled their defense as an important and stressful time even if it went well. Yet, in spite of the intensity of the experience (or perhaps because of it), many of the women could not recall in detail what they discussed. As Audrey noted, "It was kind of a blur." The formal and public presentation of their dissertation was a jarring contrast to the isolated writing they had experienced for the months or years immediately prior to the defense. During that time, the student was often alone with the dissertation, trying to mine meaning from the data or source material and write it in a cohesive and scholarly style. Finally the day arrived that these women had planned for, and they were faced with having to present and interpret, in a 20- to 30-minute period, the work they had been doing for years. And in addition, they were presenting it for the first time to faculty who were experts in their field and often eminent researchers and scholars. As noted above, Mary captured this concept with her description of the defense process:

These are your new peers, the doctorally-prepared faculty of the school that you think you're going to teach. These are the people you're going to teach with, so if you cannot be at that level of intellectual capacity, it's a pretty big signal.

End of a Journey and a New Beginning 155

Interwoven in the participants' stories was the importance of the dissertation advisor in preparing the student for the defense and in making sure that the defense process went smoothly and fairly. It was clear that some advisors had the knowledge and experience of how to do this and others were too novice or too distant to know how best to guide the student. Most people with doctorates have had only the experience of writing one dissertation. And at some point, these same women in our study who struggled to and through their defense may be dissertation advisors themselves, helping a doctoral student prepare for her or his defense. Thus the question arises: How do advisors learn their role of supervising a defense for a student? The answer is not too dissimilar to the way these women learned their role in writing the dissertation—by doing it.

Even when students are fortunate enough to have an advisor or committee who prepares them well for the defense, there can be anxiety from the unpredictability of the defense. What questions will be asked? What small thing might turn into a big sticking point for one committee member? The best, most experienced, advisor cannot fully prepare a student for these unknowns. Heraclitus declared, "Upon those who step into the same rivers, different and again different waters flow,"[1] meaning that even when an experience may be similar in key ways, it is always inescapably different. In this way, each defense is new for the advisor and committee just as it is for the student. That realization in itself may be comforting for the student. The committee has no secret knowledge about how the defense will play out, and it is up to the advisor to help the student and committee come together in mutual trust to create a defense that is challenging, fruitful, and hopefully resulting in success for the student.

In addition to addressing the issues above, in this chapter, we want to reflect on what was *not* in our participants' stories—a theme that seems oddly missing. Other than being a ritual or coronation or final hurdle, none of our participants talked about what the defense in itself might accomplish. Presumably, this gap is in part because their advisors had not discussed this question with them. None of the women appeared to conceptualize the defense process as focused on helping them think of themselves as scholars or on where their next scholarly endeavors might take them. If the purpose of writing a dissertation is to help a student become a scholar, it seems that the defense process should not only focus on endings, but on beginnings.

Since the defense is usually the first public presentation of years of research and writing by the student, it is surprising that this formal gathering of scholars is focused so intently on *defending* the research by answering questions posed by committee members, rather than having the committee members learn from the insights uncovered by the student. This focus on defending is exemplified by Greta's comment, who appreciated the good advice of her committee chair for helping her to avoid problems:

She helped me to prepare for every part of the way, to anticipate barriers and solve them before they happened to me. So we—I came to my defense with eight pages that I sent to this problematic person [on my committee] before I defended that day that answered every objection that she had. And I was well ready to defend everything.

In a public forum where expert scholars interact with a student who is presumably about to enter the formal world of scholarship, one would hope there would be intellectual curiosity on the part of the official experts not only to have their questions answered but also to find out what new questions they should be asking as a result of the student's research.

If the doctoral defense is to be a true academic experience and an opportunity for intellectual growth for all parties involved, one would hope the defense would more explicitly aim for what Gadamer terms "a fusion of horizons."[2] While Gadamer focuses his discussion of hermeneutics mainly on historical texts, his arguments apply also to any text written by someone other than oneself. In a dissertation defense, the committee asks questions about a text by an Other, a student who has different experiences, perspectives, and judgments than any of the committee members.

In a fusion of horizons, the reader recognizes that "the hermeneutical situation is determined by the prejudices that we bring with us."[3] These prejudices constitute the reader's own horizon, "beyond which it is impossible to see."[4] Each committee member, as well as the student, brings his or her own prejudices and preconceptions—his or her own horizon—to the text of the dissertation. But Gadamer argues that such a horizon is not fixed and can, in fact, move and be changed by interaction with a text or an Other:

> But now it is important to avoid the error of thinking that the horizon of the present consists of a fixed set of opinions and valuations, and that the otherness of the past [or the Other] can be foregrounded from it as from a fixed ground. In fact, the horizon of the present is continually in the process of being formed because we are continually having to test all our prejudices. . . . There is no . . . isolated horizon of the present in itself . . . Rather, understanding is always the fusion of these horizons supposedly existing by themselves. . . . In the process of understanding, a real fusing of horizons occurs—which means that, as the historical [or Other's] horizon is projected, it is simultaneously superseded.[5]

Gadamer argues that any process of understanding is a constant to-and-fro between our own present horizon and the Other's horizon, and in that very process, our present horizon becomes changed; thus the relationship between the two horizons changes, and thus our understanding must take these changes into account so that we may reinterpret our own horizons—and so continues the hermeneutic cycle. Trying to understand this cycle and to foreground consistently the changing horizonal relationships is what Gadamer calls "the central problem of hermeneutics."[6]

What would a defense explicitly structured around a fusion of horizons look like? It would be a respectful shared inquiry between parties, all interested in the same subject. Gadamer points out that a fusion of horizons does not mean the forming of one horizon, but instead a recognition that two horizons coming together can transform each other.[7] Such a transformation would require committee members to listen not just for the answers they hope to hear but for answers that may be surprising, or for new challenging questions. As Heidegger says, "It . . . might be helpful to rid ourselves of the habit of only hearing what we already understand."[8] Similarly, Gadamer notes that "anyone who listens is fundamentally open. Without this kind of openness to each other, there is no genuine human relationship. Belonging together always also means being able to listen to one another."[9]

What seems to be missing in our participants' discussion of their defense is an explicit sense of shared inquiry, of a mutual desire to reach a new understanding of the subject at hand. Mary described how she felt in the space created at her defense: "All of a sudden, you're in a space where, it's not that you're not confident, but you're not an expert." This space can be structured as a space not to intimidate but to gather learning. In fact, such a structure may present a higher and more meaningful challenge to the student, for Gadamer insists that "No text and no book speaks if it does not speak a language that reaches the other person."[10] A student's dissertation—and her presentation of it—should be able to spark an engaging discussion for a committee who is open and listening.

This fusion of horizons in a defense may focus mainly on the subject matter of the dissertation, but some committees and advisors may also want to dialogue on the meaning and significance of the students' experience writing the dissertation. The committee and the student might all benefit from taking a meta-perspective and discussing what went well or wrong in the process, or what surprised the student about the process or her findings. Doctoral advisors may want to consider which traditional practices to hold on to and which to let go as they expand conventional pedagogical approaches in an attempt to create a structure for the defense that not only requires the student to defend her acquisition of knowledge but to create a space for shared inquiry on the subject matter of the dissertation and perhaps on the process of dissertating itself.

In thinking of the defense as the end of a journey, it is important for readers to think how this milestone will set the context for a new beginning in their career and life goals. The long and stressful dissertation process is almost over, and it is important for the doctoral candidate to approach the defense with confidence and a sense of herself as a scholar. This is a never-again time when she has the opportunity to address scholars who know and have approved her work; she is the expert in this specific area of research and has the chance to share that knowledge with her committee. Readers may want to prepare for the defense by asking peers about their suggestions for ensuring that the defense is successful and perhaps even enjoyable. Also, a frank discussion with their advisor about what is expected during the defense may be helpful. The defending student may want to consider and discuss: What is my goal for the defense—other than success? What is my advisor's goal? Are there specific red flags to watch out for? Will there be an opportunity for shared inquiry between me and the committee? With careful communication before the defense about what the student would like to see happen, the committee may be open to possibilities of learning and teaching during the defense so that student and committee can begin to move toward a new understanding of each other as colleagues and co-inquirers in their academic discipline.

Chapter 7

Looking Back

Sometimes, we think that it is not in our realm, whatever it is that's ahead of us is for somebody else to do. I'm not smart enough or I'm not good enough or I'm not educated enough or I'm not, or whatever. But what I've learned is that I'm as good as the rest of them.

— Gretchen

For us, as researchers, one of the most overwhelming and powerful aspects of these interviews was listening to the participants talk about how they feel now as they look back on their dissertation experiences. These women were sometimes unable to articulate or make sense of their experiences and feelings as they were undergoing them, but now they have the perspective to interpret and analyze as they look back on their journey. The participants seemed to enjoy trying to capture a big-picture description of the dissertation and their experience with it. In this big picture, they could look back at their journey, see where it had taken them and where it had left them, and reflect on the lessons they learned along the way.

The Stories

While a dissertation experience can be challenging and even exhausting, the women we interviewed consistently said given the choice, they would do it all over again, though not necessarily the same way. Some women commented that they felt a dissertation experience has to be what each individual makes it, and that dissertation completion only happens if one makes it happen. Several of the women said that it took them a while to realize that the dissertation experience was over, that it was complete. Others commented on the emotional aftereffects, both negative and positive. And finally, several of the participants voiced desire to encourage others in their own efforts to pursue and complete doctoral degrees. Feeling empowered themselves, these women want to help others have the sense of accomplishment and the increased career opportunities that they now have.

It Was Exhausting, but I Would Do It Again

In talking about a big-picture description, Naomi was the most matter-of-fact: "The best dissertation is a *done* dissertation." She also expressed the toll the process had taken on her:

It truly, was *truly* the most exhausting thing I have ever done. More exhausting than childbirth, more exhausting than running a marathon. Wow!

Kim also spoke of the dissertation experience as something that pushed her to the limits, and she used a strikingly similar analogy to Naomi's "running a marathon":

It was an achievement, and it's like, phew (takes in an audible breath), completing a 5K run. And you've crossed the finish line, and you might not always be first, and it didn't even matter if you were last, you finished, you finished. Because in many ways I think it's a race, and like they say, not everybody comes to the starting line with all the same gifts.

Bubbles spoke not of exhaustion but of feeling ready to be done, ready to move on:

> I did feel relief—when I went to drop it off. . . . I do remember that there was a kind of, okay, you've spent so much time and so much emotional and intellectual energy on this thing, and then it turns out to be a slim volume. (Laughs) It's kind of weird, you know? But I think mostly, I was just really looking forward to what was coming next, and I was excited to move on and do other things.

We asked some of the women, "If you could go back in time and rethink your decision to pursue a doctoral degree, would you change your mind? Would you take a different path or would you do it again?" All the women we asked this of responded that yes, they would do it all over again. Naomi elided her description of how exhausting and draining the experience was with her commitment that she would do it all over again if she needed to:

> It was a very long journey. I mean, the process is so time-consuming. But I think that is how it was for everybody. I don't know, but it was a very long journey. Looking back, I can't believe how many hours of my life it took right then. What is essentially a relatively small document. I mean, it's unbelievable to me what it was. Not only was it time-consuming, I mean it literally sucked every ounce of energy out of me: physically, emotionally . . . Gosh! On the other hand, I have to say, if I had it to do over again, I would.

Audrey took this affirmation of her experience a step further, realizing that not only would she do it again, but in some ways, she missed the experience:

> *Audrey:* It was the time pressure. It was a lot to do in a short period of time. And I think it was just getting into a routine at the time that—in some ways, I really enjoyed that. I miss that state of being productive. I was sooo productive. It was because it was forced on me, and at times I was panicking,

I'll never get this done in time, but it was a productive state to be in. And it felt, in many ways, better than forcing myself to do five minutes, 15 minutes. . . .

Researcher: So you actually miss that state. You enjoyed. . . . What felt good about it?

Audrey: I think, partly, it was a feeling of being motivated, of achievement, that I could see, even in my most despairing moments, I could see that there was something that was coming together. And I could see that it was going to get there.

Suzy certainly did not regret her time writing her dissertation, but looking back, she did think that perhaps the experience—for her and for others—could be made somewhat less daunting. Even though she felt she had an excellent advisor, she wished somehow advisors could guide each student to design a research study that would result in a quality dissertation but yet suit each individual's personality and goals:

I had a great advisor who would read what I wrote and give me very helpful comments and keep pushing me in the right direction but I think it might have been easier if at some point early on in the process they would have said, "You can make this easier, or you can make it difficult, but for you, your personality, your goal, your subject matter, your program of research, whatever, for you, let's go on *this* path so that you can learn without aggravating yourself." Because I really think there's a really hard way to do this, and yeah, you learn a lot, but the level of aggravation gets so high that maybe we could learn what we need without that. And maybe somewhere early on in the dissertation process, yes, we talk about whether this is feasible, but really looking at a very practical way, "How feasible is this without totally aggravating you and yet having a rigorous and meaningful project?" I think that's not an easy thing for an advisor, or a student to do, but maybe there should be more emphasis on that. . . . Advisors and academics are researchers themselves, and I fully appreciate the passion for that being conveyed to the student, and that can be good, but sometimes, they are so much higher than the students, and they think, "Oh, I know, you can add this question and that question," and the student goes, "Okay, sure, sure"—and then you end up with 37 research questions. And the feasibility of doing this well within the time frame of a couple of years can be overwhelming.

The Strong Importance of Personal Commitment

Looking back, many of the women spoke of the dissertation process as something they just had to make themselves do. They had to make the dissertation process their own, and simply commit to it as a part of their life for however long the process took. They realize now that their success was largely due to their unwillingness to give up. Interestingly, some of these same women talked about how *unhelpful* they found it while they were dissertating when peers, advisors, or family would say to them, "You just have to get it done." Thus, it seems that this advice, although it seemed unhelpful at the time, might actually be true.

Kim found that she relied on her own commitment to keep going and to do something that mattered:

I always felt that in the end you have to look at yourself in the mirror and ask, "Did I do anything that mattered?" And so you keep going. And I think that's part of life. You are always going to be handed obstacles, and you always are going to have to answer, "How bad do I want this?" and so you, or, "Is it time to stop?" That's what I struggled with.

While Alecia said she had sometimes fantasized about quitting the whole dissertation process, going back to work, and never mentioning the whole thing ever again, she realized she was not willing to let herself get so far and then walk away with nothing. She also noted that while the support of her committee and friends was helpful, in the end, it was her own commitment that mattered:

There were moments when I would think that, like even when I first got to [school name], I remember thinking that if there was a way that I could just show up back in my old job at home, and nobody would ask me any questions, I would do it. But I knew there was no way I could just show up . . . (laughs) you know, back on the ladder. So, by the time we got this far ahead, it was the same thing. If there was a way that I could just turn back the clock, an alternate timeline, and start off on the track heading the same way, the way I hadn't done it, you know, that would be a nice option, but I also knew there was no way that . . . like I had come too far in this process, I wasn't walking out with nothing. I could understand all too well how people got to that, because just that whole . . . just before, when you have this all in your head and you've got to put this proposal together, it's overwhelming.

You know, I think it's interesting because you have this committee, and I think support matters, but ultimately, the dissertation is a solo event, 'cause ultimately, it's what you put on that paper that counts. And it's what your thoughts are, and how you analyze and organize the end result. And so the support's wonderful, all the people who you talked to about it are wonderful, but ultimately, and which, I think, is what happens with a lot of people . . . I think it's hard to commit to sitting at that computer and actually putting it down, 'cause that's how it's solely done at that point.

Greta worried that students just embarking in doctoral programs would be discouraged by the frustrations and concerns expressed by students further along in the program. She defended her doctoral program and tried to shift the conversation to personal commitment and knowledge of one's own strengths and capabilities:

Ya know, it's interesting because I know so many bad stories. And some students were sitting in here for this conference when I had my friend who's thinking about doctoral education, I almost hate for her—and I said to her yesterday, "I hate for you to hear all these bad things." I loved my program. I mean I loved, I—I had—it was good for me—but it was not magic. I worked hard to make sure it ended up the way I wanted it to be. And that's, ya know—it takes hard work. And knowing what's—knowing yourself and what you don't do well.

Is It Over? Am I Done?

Several of the women laughed or expressed frustration and bewilderment at their own inability to realize when the whole process was over. Claire joked that she had thought it was over, then panicked and realized it was not over, but really it was:

> My school had this superstition that if you walked over the big school seal that was in the floor, you'd never graduate. Well, after my defense, I was so giddy to be out of there, I just walked right over that seal. I think I did a little skip, actually. Then, later when I needed to Fed-Ex my dissertation to officially file it—I was cutting it close because it had taken me so long to get the formatting right—my husband and I are driving to the Fed-Ex place, and we got a flat tire. A flat tire! It's like 4:15, and I'm panicking, and all I could think was, "I shouldn't have walked on the seal." Which is of course totally irrational, but that's what I couldn't get out of my head. But we were able to get the tire fixed in time, and I did file on time. And only then did I really, really feel like it was all over. I had done it. And I think it took me quite a while after that to really believe it.

Naomi also had trouble realizing she was done. She had trouble shaking the habits of thought developed during that long process—waiting for feedback, meeting due dates, revising:

> Even when it was done, it didn't feel done. I kept waiting for somebody to tell me I had something else due. Even when I defended the dissertation, when it was over, and I'm so exhausted! And I remember them saying, "Okay, it's done, Naomi." But, there is a final comment. They handed me, you know, like sticky notes. They handed me like a one-hundred page document or whatever, and they had sticky notes, and they were like, "You're done!" Okay, if you're giving me sticky notes, then I'm not done. And I remember thinking, I will never be done, this will *never* be over!

Mary had trouble realizing the process was over because she did not perceive a clear break between her dissertation writing and her need to publish in her field:

I haven't quite finished 'cause I haven't published anything yet. I've defended; I have the diploma, I'm all good to go, but I still have . . . I'm presenting my results at a conference in June at the state level, and then I have an article that I'm working on. So the dissemination of the results is kind of the final stage of the dissertation process. It's a continuum of knowledge attainment or discernment or creation, really.

Audrey's story about how she felt when it was all supposedly over was the most powerful and emotional story we encountered on the subject. She did not want to let her dissertation go until it was perfect, and then when she really had to admit it was done, she felt strangely let down:

> *Audrey:* When I filed, I phoned my friend and I said, "Is it over?" And she said, "Yes, yes, it's in!"
> *Researcher:* You needed to hear that?
> *Audrey:* Oh, yes, I was crying. The letdown was just awful. And you know the woman who took it from me at the filing office had to pry it out of my fingers, because I didn't want to let it go, and my advisor *helpfully* mentioned some footnote that was missing off my final version, and I thought, I want three minutes to fix this! And then I thought no, no, let's just. . . .

It was such a letdown. It really was. I sat down, and I cried. I actually sat down, there was a statue of [the school's founder] on campus next to the office where the dissertations were filed, and I walked out like a zombie, and I sat down underneath the feet of the statue, and I just started bawling. I really, I just felt so let down and so tense from the whole situation. And it doesn't happen—there's no point where it stops, and they throw you a party. It was the defense when they were going to pass it, and then there was the final version that was handed in, and then there was my graduation date at the end of the semester, and then there was the actual graduation. So it was so spun out in these stages that there was no point at which I felt I could sit down and go, "Yes, it's really done now."

I think a lot of it was actually continued anxiety—I couldn't let it go. I was worried about what it still might say. And everyone says, well, nobody reads your dissertation, but it really isn't true anymore. In fact, I had just signed the agreement that let them put it online, and when it was online, it actually was read by hundreds of people—at least hundreds of people have downloaded it, I don't know if they've actually read it. It's out there—it's got my name on it—and anything stupid that it says can be attributed to me. So I had this whole anxiety. I was really concentrated on that footnote. That missing footnote, or maybe it was incorrect—it was something really dumb, that nobody would ever notice apart from me and my advisor. But I was—I had this continued sense that this wasn't finished, that there was something wrong with it, that I needed more time, and then the lady pried it away from me and threw it on a shelf, she did, she threw it on the shelf behind her, and I reached for her hands and I tried. . . . (Laughs)

Researcher: I can't imagine just seeing it tossed like that!
Audrey: She tossed it in a box and threw it on the shelf, yeah. So, yeah, there was a lot of continued anxiety. And there was a little bit of, "What the eff do I do now?" because it consumed my life for so long. And I was at the printer that morning, so everything I'd been concentrating on, and everything I'd been doing was suddenly taken away from me. And I just felt direction-less. And I knew that I should be happy, and part of me kind of blamed myself for not being happy, but I should have been skipping down the street, and I was crying. I thought, you know, here's this great achievement that my mom thinks is the most wonderful thing ever, and I'm sobbing over it!

As Audrey notes here, because a student moves from dissertation completion to defense to filing to commencement, there really is no clear point at which one can stop and celebrate. The defense seems too early, filing happens quietly, and commencement is often well after the fact, when the now-no-longer-student is back to work or out on the job market, having moved on to the next phase of her life.

Emotional Aftereffects

The strong emotions of letdown and lack of direction that Audrey felt when she realized it was over are similar to some of the more general emotional aftereffects other women found upon completion of their doctoral degree. Naomi said that she had never entirely recovered from the process:

> [I succeeded], but I still have PTSD! I swear (laughs), I have flashbacks! A friend of mine, um, from the PhD program, we talk about it. I run into her at the gym, and we start talking about the PTSD program. It's like I have sweating, and I get almost sick to my stomach. It's like a PTSD, a PTSD flashback! And she feels the exact same way. I just think it's such a shame that that process sort of leaves everyone feeling completely rung out for *years*.

Stella reported quite pleasant memories of the dissertation process, saying, "Generally I found the dissertation process somewhat pleasurable . . . I thought it was really, that it was really fun." But she also admitted such memories sometimes overlooked the harder times:

> I'm not entirely remembering the parts where I was feeling crushed, as there was this time, someone asked how it was going, I said, "Oh, pretty good, I'm working on the acknowledgments, I'm working on the acknowledgments for my advisor right now, how do you say 'soul crusher,' or what's a euphemism for 'soul crushing'?" It was only halfway joking. But if he had come up with a really good euphemism for soul crushing, I would have included it (laughs).

Bubbles found that her dissertation and post-doctoral research left her with a crisis of identity. Although she enjoyed the research and writing of her dissertation, she began to realize as she completed it that the goal she wanted, to work as a biology researcher, now seemed hollow to her:

I don't really know if I would have done anything differently, because everything I did got me where I am now, which I'm very, very, very happy, so it's hard to say that, you know, anything wasn't—that I misplaced my time or energy in any way.

Part of the reason I'm at a teaching institution now is that I had this growing—I called it a crisis of identity about doing research, and how it's very esoteric, this thing. And I just really would say, once I started my post-doc, because I thought I'm burned out, I'm tired of doing this, I'm going to move on, and then when I moved on, that feeling instead of subsiding, just sort of kept increasing in my brain—what are you doing to make the world a better place? That was really the continual thing I was feeling. Part of the thing that I didn't like about being a scientist was going to these meetings where, I shouldn't say this because it sounds mean, but a lot of people just have a very inflated sense of their own self-worth. It's like, you're doing this thing that nobody gives a shit about, and somehow, you've pumped yourself up to be the hero of crickets. It became kind of absurd to me, the thing I was doing became absurd in some ways. Even though there's a part of me that did then and still now really thinks it's neat, but just being neat wasn't good enough anymore for me to justify the sort of blood, sweat, and tears and everything you give up to be a successful scientist. Because I mean quite frankly, if you're a successful science researcher at an institution, you have no life. I mean, you just have no other life. And I just felt like, I don't want to be that person. So I do think that it became—I did two post-docs, and they were both research—I was trying to give myself another chance to do this because you feel like I invested all this time and I can't think now that this is something I don't want to do, that's ridiculous. But then I realized, you have to stop kidding yourself. I cannot see myself doing this. And then I just started exploring other alternative things, and that was a little bit painful to do, even though in my eyes, I didn't go that far afield from what I wanted to do.

Bubbles realizes that she has disappointed her mentors and peers who saw her as such a talented researcher:

In the eyes of the very supportive people that were my mentors, being at a teaching college is like, you just gave up. What's wrong with you? Like you're a failure . . . I think that my mentor, I think in a lot of ways he thought that I was sort of a protégé for him, and it was a little bit, I think, maybe he took it personally, or it was a little bit hurtful personally, but before I ever got the job I have now, I said, "I don't want to do this anymore." And I mean he really tried, "You don't mean that, and you're just, you know, whatever," and really I think he just couldn't believe it. But I do think it was a good decision, and I've never been as happy as I am now. . . . And I think the last time that I saw everyone, I think many of them mentioned that I seem very, very happy, and I think it finally crystalized for them that there's a lot of ways that you can define success.

Thus, even though she was left troubled and questioning by her years of devotion to research, Bubbles was still able to find a path leading from her dissertation to a life that now makes her very happy.

More than any of the other women we interviewed, Gretchen and Greta reported quite positive emotional aftereffects from the dissertation process. Gretchen found she had a new professional identity and standing, and she could be proud of herself:

I immediately was Dr. Myers. The next week I came to class, and my students celebrated with me. . . . I was immediately Dr. Myers, but I would always do a double take whenever I heard it. It was kinda like using "Mrs." after you get married . . . only this is like, "Wow! I really did it!" That was the feeling. (laughing) It was, "I did it!" Thank you to my husband, my children, to my colleagues for supporting me, so I was very grateful. I was proud of myself. I could see that my students were proud of me.

Greta expressed similar pride in herself, realizing her sense of accomplishment in a job well done and the lessons she had learned in the process:

You know, I learned all these little lessons along the way. So you know—I'm just—I must have done it pretty good. So there must have been some little things I picked up along the way.

When she looked back on her accomplishment, Gretchen confessed that until she completed her doctoral degree, she had held others above her, thinking they were better than her. Now that she was finished, she realized she was as good as those around her:

Um, now I could I see that I am, um, as good as anybody else. And I see *that* after going to meeting after meeting, and listening to what other people are saying, and seeing how they are responding to issues in their schools. You know how you sorta hold people up here? (Gestures above head) And then up higher, at a higher level, wow! That must be really great! I don't know if I could ever go there or be there or do that. Um, and maybe it's, I don't know if it's the confidence from being 50-something or if it's the confidence that the education gave me, or if it's the confidence doing a job like this. Maybe it's all of the above, but um, much more confidence. I think that's actually the words of my husband, "What a difference in your confidence!"

There was pride when I was finished, and I have to say he made the observation about confidence, but I also made the observation as well. Sometimes, we think that that is not in our realm, whatever it is that's ahead of us is for somebody else to do. I'm not smart enough, or I'm not good enough, or I'm not educated enough, or I'm not, or whatever. But what I've learned is that I'm as good as the rest of them.

Encouraging Others

Perhaps because of these positive outcomes and emotions that Greta and Gretchen felt looking back on their experiences, they now go out of their way in their own lives to encourage others who want to pursue a doctoral degree. Gretchen specifically wants to encourage others at her workplace who want to go on for PhDs:

And I want to do the same thing for them that I felt when I was going to school. It doesn't make it any less hard, it's still hard, but there's something about people coming up to you and saying, "You go, Girl!"

In encouraging others, Greta said she specifically wants to follow her committee chair's good model of introducing people and connecting them with others who can help them because Greta appreciated very much when her chair had done that for her.

Um, I think a good chair connects people. [Another chair I know] made sure she introduced her pre-doc students . . . to all the people that they needed to know. So you know helping to connect them. And you know I mean [my chair] did do that for me by lending me—she let me use her name. But you know, personally introducing people and bringing them into the world where they're going to go to. You know I've tried to do that now—when I'm presenting something—like even today at this conference, I'm bringing Susan along, and I try to introduce her to people. Susan's thinking about going for a doctorate, and so I mentioned something to the school where she's thinking of going to and told them about Susan and then said, "Well, Susan, I told them about you, so when you call them they know about you because I've already told them about you"—I mean that's what a good chair does kind of—some of that political work—background work . . . And so I'd like to have everybody have a smooth journey. And to help people along the way.

In addition to Gretchen and Greta, Martha also wants to encourage others who want to pursue a doctoral degree, particularly in her field:

Well, I'd say [to anyone who wants to do this], first of all, you know, you can do it. And if it seems like it's miserable, okay, but you know, it'll get better. But if you spend time and think it through and sit down and talk with somebody who has been through the process, who can help you think it through, your project, your process, and do as much up-front planning as you can, then you'll, I think you'll be very successful.

One perhaps should not read too much into this last line, but it is interesting to note that Martha corrects herself here. She seems to start to say "You'll be successful," but changes it to "I think you'll be successful." Perhaps she wishes that anyone can be successful who wants to be, but realizes that wish cannot be a promise, given everything she knows about the struggle that got her where she is today—finished with her doctoral degree.

Reflections on the Stories

We hope that in this chapter and in the book as a whole, our readers can see the personal and professional growth these women accomplished through the act of writing their dissertations. Some women were happy with their experiences, some were simply happy to have made it through. But even if one's attitude is as pragmatic and frank as Naomi's, that "the best dissertation is a done dissertation," that accomplishment—that being done—can still shine as a gift that opens up a personal and professional life that would likely not have been possible otherwise. Friedrich Nietzsche famously said, "What does not kill me makes me stronger."[1] This statement is not some trite encouragement to pick oneself up, brush oneself off, and move on. The statement represents a deep commitment to the belief that each of us is always growing, always becoming. In that growth, each of us shapes whom she becomes, perhaps especially through the most difficult times. And as long as those most difficult times help her better accomplish and achieve who she wants to be, Nietzsche believes a person can and should embrace those times. He captures this belief most vividly with a story:

What if some day or night a demon were to steal into your loneliest loneliness and say to you: "This life as you now live it and have lived it you will have to live once again and innumerable times again; and there will be nothing new in it, but every pain and every joy and every thought and sigh and everything unspeakably small or great in your life must return to you, all in the same succession and sequence . . ." Would you not throw yourself down and gnash your teeth and curse the demon who spoke thus? Or have you once experienced a tremendous moment when you would have answered him: ". . . never have I heard anything more divine." . . . How well disposed would you have to become to yourself and to life *to long for nothing more fervently* than for this ultimate eternal confirmation and seal?[2]

Perhaps nearly anyone who has written a doctoral dissertation understands the phrase, "your loneliest loneliness." What if, at our most vulnerable time, our most desperate, lonely time, we were offered the gift (the curse?) that all we are living might happen again and again? Nietzsche encourages each of us to have the strength to say joyfully, "Yes, I would do it all again." And the reason a person can say that is because of how well disposed she has become to herself. That which does not kill us makes us stronger. If the challenges, frustrations, and (hopefully) joys of the dissertation experience help someone become what she wants to be, that happiness of self helps her embrace everything she went through to get there. Perhaps this is one reason why, so consistently, when we asked participants "Would you do it all again if you had the choice?" each said yes, she would.

Nietzsche and other existentialists teach that for each person, her story is what she makes it. Each of us chooses how to understand, interpret, and define the journey of her life. The women in our book might see triumphs where others see small accomplishments, and they might see failures where others would be most impressed. Each woman's story is her own story, and that story is the truth for her. As Simone de Beauvoir said, "Because I offer no judgment of myself, I feel no resistance to speaking frankly about my own life and myself, at least, in so far as I place myself within my own universe. Perhaps my image projected in a different world . . . might disconcert or embarrass me. But so long as it is I who paint my own portrait, nothing daunts me."[3]

We hope we have helped preserve each woman's voice to let her tell her own story, paint her own self-portrait. As we look back on our research, after speaking with these women and spending countless hours working closely with interview transcriptions, we have come to feel that we know each of these women quite well: Celeste's frankness ("It'll kick your butt"), Mary's determination, Eleanor's beautiful descriptions of feeling lost and looking for hope, Bubbles' ability to laugh at herself, Audrey's courage in talking about raw emotions, and Greta's and Gretchen's capacity to find so many positives in their dissertation experiences. Even though we had nothing to do with these women's accomplishments, we find pride in their successes nonetheless, and we join them in their wish to encourage others considering the pursuit of a doctoral degree. As Greta said, "I'd like to have everybody have a smooth journey. And to help people along the way."

Appendix

Gathering the Stories

Saying to a fellow student, I'm feeling like I really can't cope, and hearing, "I feel the same way," it sort of relieves a lot and makes you realize maybe you're not as abnormal as you perceive yourself to be.

— Callie

The stories in this book are from 20 women who, at the time of their interviews, were currently dissertating or had completed a dissertation within the last four years. These women wrote doctoral dissertations across nine disciplines—biology, English literature, modern languages, history, mathematics, music, nursing, philosophy, and social work. Despite the significantly different nature of dissertations in these fields, we were consistently struck by the similarities between the experiences of the women we interviewed. It seems that much of the journey of writing a dissertation has little to do with the actual disciplinary content of the work and more to do with the challenges and transformations in the writer's own identity and her relationships.

Our participants were two African-American women and 18 white women, including two international students from English-speaking countries; the participants as a group ranged from ages 29–55 at the time of their interviews. Some of the details and all of the names in these stories have been changed to preserve anonymity. In most cases, the research participant chose her own pseudonym, picking a name that suited her personality or that she had always wanted to be called. (The participant referred to as "Bubbles" laughed as she confessed, "I've always wanted to be called Bubbles. Will you call me Bubbles in the book?") While these details have been changed, the stories are real. All quotations in this book are from women who shared with us stories of writing a doctoral dissertation through the lenses of their own lived experience.

Each participant signed an informed consent form that detailed the structure and purpose of the study. We encouraged our participants to be as open and frank with us as they were comfortable being. Some of the stories reveal troubling issues with advisors or sensitive discussions with spouses, so we are grateful to our participants for trusting us with their stories. They have trusted us not only to protect their anonymity but also to represent to the best of our ability their thoughts authentically and in context so that their voices might be heard and shared with others going through similar experiences.

In the process of conducting these interviews, we thought of the women not as research participants but as co-inquirers, all of us working together to unravel the mysteries, frustrations, and triumphs of the dissertation experience. We used a hybrid approach in the interviews, sometimes asking questions to call forth long narratives, sometimes engaging in dialogue and pressing our participants with follow-up questions or challenges. Our goal was to help each woman reflect on her own beliefs and access ideas and assumptions she may not have thought about before. We also wanted to give each participant a chance to tell the stories that meant the most to her or that she felt best represented key phases in her dissertation experience.

Appendix: Gathering the Stories

In studying the phenomenon that is the dissertation experience, we recognize that each person's dissertation experience is her own, and thus we sought to understand each woman's experience through her own perceptions and her own voice. Our hybrid approach of stories and dialogue, combined with our commitment to welcoming our participants as co-inquirers, yielded the rich and diverse stories that fill this book.

Research Approach

The research question for our study was: "What is the lived experience of a woman writing a doctoral dissertation?" Our research approach was influenced primarily by the works of the philosophers Socrates, Heidegger, and Gadamer. According to Heidegger and Gadamer, if one wishes to study and interpret a phenomenon, one should seek not a method but a mode of understanding. In his *Truth and Method*, Gadamer argues:

> Given the intermediate position in which hermeneutics operates, it follows that its work is not to develop a procedure of understanding, but to clarify the conditions in which understanding takes place. But these conditions do not amount to a "procedure" or method which the interpreter must of himself bring to bear on the text; rather, they must be given.[1]

Similarly, Heidegger rejects the idea of a set, pre-determined method because "every inquiry is a seeking," and "every seeking gets guided before-hand by what is sought."[2]

We wanted to allow ourselves to be guided by what we sought even as the phenomenon under investigation changed and morphed depending on each individual woman's experience, so we allowed our mode of interaction and questioning to change from interview to interview or within the same interview, depending on where the inquiry was going and what seemed to work best for each participant. Heidegger and Gadamer both argue that the inquirer is always at the same time interpreter, and the interpreter has memories and experiences that will inevitably shape the interpretation. Therefore, one should not pretend to shut out these influences, since they cannot be shut out. Heidegger even suggests that what the seeker already knows about what is sought must inform her decision as to what question to formulate.[3] Therefore, we remained aware that we, the researchers, have ourselves experienced the process of writing a doctoral dissertation, and we sometimes allowed that experience to inform our choice of questions or responses.

Since any experience, and perhaps especially an experience like writing a dissertation, is always a person's own, we sought to understand what the phenomenologist Husserl calls the "lived experience" of each woman we interviewed.[4] We wanted to help each participant describe vividly her own lived experience, complete with the richness of details, context, and emotions that originally shaped that experience. Yet experience is always immediate and complex, and thus it is elusive when one tries to recall it. Thus, it can be difficult for any description to capture its essence.[5] Our flexible interviewing approach let us try to help each woman recall and describe her lived experience in the way that would work best for her.

Narratives and Dialogue

When we wished to call forth a long narrative, we asked about a "critical incident" that had particularly stood out to the participant.[6] In such cases, we avoided interrupting or prompting any more than necessary, trying to allow the women's stories to develop and unfold organically. Human beings are story-driven creatures,[7] and we often see our own lives narratively. Thus, asking someone to tell a story about the best time she remembers, or the worst, or the most frightening, or the most surprising, can help bring out ideas, assumptions, beliefs, and reactions that might not come up in response to back-and-forth questioning. In addition, we hoped these longer stories would be cathartic for the women telling them and would allow our readers to get a sense of these women's personalities and lived experiences through their own voices.

For the bulk of each interview, between these narratives, we engaged in dialogue with our participants, using the method of Socratic-Hermeneutic Shared Inquiry.[8] We followed participants' responses with questions that pressed them further or dug deeper into their thoughts and experiences. In hermeneutics, any answer leads to more questions, and therefore, Gadamer argues, "the hermeneutic phenomenon . . . implies the primacy of dialogue."[9] In a dialogue, any question can lead to unexpected paths, or it can be challenged or even rejected by the researcher or the participant. The flexibility of a dialogue allows the questions to be led by the participant's answers and by what has been revealed of the phenomenon so far. The questions can be led by what Heidegger calls "the inconspicuous guide who takes us by the hand—or better said, by the word—in . . . conversation."[10]

In order to engage in fruitful dialogue with our participants, we followed primarily the lead of Socrates, whose principles of inquiry come to us through the writings of his greatest student, Plato. Like Heidegger, Socrates perceived and respected the inconspicuous guide in an investigative conversation: He maintained that "the lover of inquiry must follow his beloved wherever it may lead him."[11] Socrates also believed that when investigating a phenomenon, one should always start with a definition. If he wanted to learn about friendship, he would start with "what is friendship?" If he wanted to learn about justice, he would start with "what is justice?" Such definitional questions, he believed, needed to take precedence over questions *about* the phenomenon under investigation. One cannot investigate how it feels to be in a friendship before one knows what friendship really is, and one cannot look into whether it is good to be just before one knows what justice is.[12] Similarly, we did not want to ask our participants what their dissertation experience had been like for them without first establishing what they believed a dissertation to be. Participants often found it difficult at first to provide a definition, but they seemed to enjoy and learn from the effort. In fact, participants often returned of their own accord to attempting a definition once again, wanting to tie the ongoing discussion back to their own desire for a definition.

Throughout each interview process, we also kept in mind Socrates' "say what you believe" requirement. Socrates believed that since each person must search for truths within herself, it is pointless to consider what others might think or say on a given topic, and a co-inquirer must speak her mind and be honest with herself and her dialogue partner. Even though we were not seeking truths, *per se*, we did want the women we interviewed to look inside themselves to explore their own thoughts and experiences and not to worry about what other people thought or what they perceived we might want them to say. We thus encouraged our participants to speak their minds honestly and frankly so that the inquiry could remain true to the real experiences of the women who lived them.

In our conversations, we tried to keep in mind Socrates' image of philosophical dialogue as a way of midwifing understanding. In his life in ancient Greece, Socrates believed that he was on a mission from the god Apollo to help the citizens of Athens find the wisdom and truth each of them carried inside their own souls. Socrates described himself as a midwife in his relationship with his co-inquirers. In Athens, midwives not only helped women in the birthing process; they also helped make promising matches between men and women. Socrates explained to his friend Theaetetus that like a midwife, he wished to help those who are pregnant with ideas so that those ideas might be nurtured to full term and delivered. Also like a midwife, he knew which couplings of ideas were likely to produce fertile offspring.[13]

We, too, tried to act as midwives-of-ideas and help our participants match their own beliefs against each other to compare them or mate them to see what other ideas might be birthed. Just as in Socrates' own dialogues, sometimes this process required us to point out apparent conflicts between two things the participant had said. Other times, we offered analogies or examples to tease out the implications or hidden meanings in what they had said. Socrates believed that such a process of questioning and challenging allowed the co-inquirer to turn her soul toward the truths to be found inside herself.[14]

When an apparent conflict between beliefs or statements came up, we would bring it to the attention of the participant and try to sort out the conflict by exploring the relevant issues to find out how they all fit together. When questions struck our participants as off base or not going where they wanted to go, the dialogue format allowed them, as our co-inquirers, to reshape the inquiry by rejecting or rephrasing our questions. For instance, when we asked Audrey, "Is there a particular incident during that last part of the process that stands out to you when you were really happy or really feeling like, yes, I'm enjoying this?", Audrey responded, "You know, the moments I remember best are not my moments. They're the moments of the people that I was with who were—most of the other girls graduated before I did, and it was the sense of someone else coming back victorious that was fantastic."

We sometimes asked the women about ideals—what they saw as an ideal dissertation or as an ideal relationship with an advisor. Asking about ideals allowed our participants to compare their ideals with their actual experiences, which sometimes helped them understand their frustrations and other times made them realize that the reality had been closer to the ideal than they had thought before reflecting on the matter, as we found with Callie:

> *Researcher:* I wanted to switch to what's hopefully a fun question, now that you've gone through all these anxieties

with me and everything! If I asked you what an ideal dissertation experience is, for you, is it possible to articulate that?

Callie: I think what I was talking about in my supervision meeting last week, having that bouncing around of ideas and sharing and learning and—you know, you're so stimulated, you feel fantastic. That's one of the ideals. I did actually—and it's been a fantastic experience—when I went to one of the conferences, some of my research participants were there, so one of my supervisors said, "Do your presentation for them." My immediate reaction was "No! Oh *God!* No!" But I did it. And the response was brilliant. It was absolutely brilliant. They were like, "Oh God, we can't say anything more." It was—they really enjoyed, I think, knowing—'cause I thought, they're not going to want to know. They're not going to want to know about *Gadamer*. But they did. And they wanted to know, and they asked me questions, and that was a really significant—I think it probably, getting back to myself, it's about validation I suppose, a lot of this, as well as the supervisory meeting, and this kind of feedback and reflection. And about this—what I said about authenticity, this was really important to me. So making sure that it was authentic, getting back—and they felt very well represented with what I was doing. And that's one of my key goals within it, that—I'm achieving well, and *they* think I'm achieving well, and I'm being authentic.

Researcher: Well that's exciting, because it sounds like you're moving toward a place where your experience is actually matching your vision of an ideal.

Callie: Oh, absolutely.

THE HERMENEUTIC CIRCLE AND *APORIA*

No matter what types of questions we asked or what examples or analogies we offered, we invited our participants to travel with us on the hermeneutic circle—a path of inquiry that is deliberately and fruitfully circular. We therefore asked some of the same questions more than once of the same participant and retraced our conversational steps with each participant to see what might have been overlooked the first time through. Often, ideas seemed to come back of their own accord during an interview, even when not obviously relevant to the question at hand, suggesting that the beliefs and issues were interconnected and perhaps the relationship between them needed further exploration.

This hermeneutic circle expanded as we conducted more interviews, asking similar questions of the later participants or new questions that had been prompted by the responses of earlier participants. In our earliest interviews, some similar ideas seemed to circle among the participants: the dissertation as a deep hole or inescapable trap; the communication obstacles between student and advisor; and the importance of commitment and certain moral values in the dissertation process. This pattern then suggested to us important questions to pursue in future interviews.

Another key part of this hermeneutic process is *aporia*, usually defined as a lack of resolution that leaves a longing in the inquirer. The best-known examples of *aporia* appear in Plato's Socratic dialogues, which infamously tend to end with Socrates saying some version of "let's try this one more time" and his interlocutor saying, effectively, "I have this thing I have to go do. Sorry." Thus, Plato's readers and Socrates himself are left wanting the inquiry to go on and wondering where it might lead. In phenomenological research, this *aporia* can be helpful to researcher and participant alike. The participant is likely to continue to ponder the relevant experiences, coming to a greater and deeper understanding of them, perhaps even influencing her attitudes or plans from that point. The researcher is called to ponder the phenomenon and the interview itself, considering what she wishes could have been answered, or what else she wishes she had asked. She may notice connections beginning to appear between certain ideas. By paying careful attention to this aporetic experience after each of our interviews, we allowed the inquiry itself to be our "inconspicuous guide," letting the questions that were left hanging after one interview guide us in our upcoming interviews.

Analysis of the Interviews, Interpretation of the Stories

In our chosen method of Socratic-Hermeneutic Shared Inquiry, the processes of interviewing and interpreting are not entirely separate. Much of the listening, interpreting, and connecting of ideas happens during the interviews. The more the interpretation occurs during the interview and the more the interview and interpretation become intertwined, "the more genuinely hermeneutic the research will be."[15] In the process of talking with these inspiring women and working closely with their stories, we ourselves were transformed in our views of what writing a dissertation is like and what it means. As Gadamer says of dialogue partners:

> In a successful conversation they both come under the influence of the truth of the object and are thus bound to one another in a new community. To reach an understanding in a dialogue is . . . a matter of . . . being transformed into a communion in which we do not remain what we were.[16]

We recorded each of our interviews and then transcribed them verbatim. Each of us then read the interviews and marked them to identify key ideas and themes. We both wrote comments and interpretations independently for each interview. Then, through our own shared inquiry, the two of us discussed the interviews together, either in person or through phone, Skype, or email. After recurrent discussions, we determined the main themes that we believed best reflected our participants' responses. The focus of each of the preceding chapters reflects the primary themes that we heard from our women participants. Through all of these chapters, we hope our readers were able to hear the voices of our 20 women participants, sometimes frustrated, sometimes confused, sometimes triumphant, as they reflected on the phenomenon of writing a dissertation.

Notes

Prelims

1. Alasdair C MacIntyre, *After Virtue: A Study in Moral Theory* (Notre Dame, Ind.: University of Notre Dame Press, 2007).
2. Barry Lopez, *Crow and Weasel* (San Francisco, CA: North Point Press, 1990), 48.

1 Writing the Unknown

1. Lewis Carroll, *Alice's Adventures in Wonderland* (Wellesley, MA: Branden Books, 1929), 75.
2. Plato, *Meno*, in *Five Dialogues*, 2nd ed., trans. G. M. A. Grube (Indianapolis: Hackett, 2002), 80d.
3. Ibid., 86c.
4. Plato, *Theaetetus*, trans. M. J. Levett and M. Burnyeat (Indianapolis: Hackett, 1990), 150d.

2 Mystery, Confusion, Isolation

1. Martin Heidegger, *Discourse on Thinking*, trans. John M. Anderson and E. Hans Freund (New York: Harper Torchbooks, 1969), 55.
2. Ibid., 46.
3. Ibid., 47.
4. Ibid., 59.
5. Ibid., 53.
6. Ibid., 56.
7. Ibid., 60.
8. Ibid., 47.

3 REALIGNING RELATIONSHIPS

1. Carol Gilligan, *In a Different Voice: Psychological Theory and Women's Development* (Cambridge, Mass.: Harvard University Press, 1982).
2. Mary Catherine Bateson, *Full Circles, Overlapping Lives: Culture and Generation in Transition* (New York: Random House, 2000), 3.
3. Ibid., 136.
4. Alfred North Whitehead, *Process and Reality: An Essay in Cosmology* (New York: The Free Press, 1982).

4 TRANSFORMATION OF THE SELF

1. Mary Catherine Bateson, *Full Circles, Overlapping Lives: Culture and Generation in Transition* (New York: Random House, 2000), 135.
2. Jean-Paul Sartre, "Existentialism is a Humanism," in *Existentialism from Dostoyevsky to Sartre*, ed. Walter Kaufman, trans. Philip Mairet (New York: Penguin, 1975), 348.
3. Ibid.
4. Edith Stein, *On the Problem of Empathy*, 3rd revised ed., trans. Waltraut Stein (Washington, DC: ICS, 1989), 88.
5. Ibid., 18.
6. Ibid., 88.
7. Ibid., 89.

5 ADVISOR AND COMMITTEE: DANCING WITH STRANGERS

1. Hannah Arendt, "Labor, Work, Action," in *The Portable Hannah Arendt*, ed. Peter Baehr (New York: Penguin Classics, 2003), 180.
2. Ibid., 180.
3. Ibid., 181.

6 End of a Journey and a New Beginning

1. Heraclitus, fragments, in *Readings in Ancient Greek Philosophy: From Thales to Aristotle*, 4th ed., ed. S. Marc Cohen, Patricia Curd, and C.D.C. Reeve (Indianapolis: Hackett, 2011), 34.
2. Hans-Georg Gadamer, *Truth and Method*, 2nd revised ed., trans. Joel Weinsheimer and Donald G. Marshall (New York: Continuum, 2004), 306.
3. Ibid., 306.
4. Ibid., 306.
5. Ibid., 306–7.
6. Ibid., 307.
7. Ibid., 307.
8. Martin Heidegger, "The Nature of Language," in *On the Way to Language*, trans. Peter Hertz (New York: Harper & Row, 1971), 58.
9. Hans-Georg Gadamer, *Truth and Method*, 2nd revised ed., trans. Joel Weinsheimer and Donald G. Marshall (New York: Continuum, 2004), 324.
10. Ibid., 397.

7 Looking Back

1. Friedrich Nietzsche, *The Anti-Christ, Ecce Homo, Twilight of the Idols, And Other Writings*, ed. Aaron Ridley, trans. Judith Norman (New York: Cambridge UP, 2005), 157.
2. Friedrich Nietzsche, *The Gay Science: With a Prelude in German Rhymes and an Appendix of Songs*, ed. Bernard Williams, trans. Josefine Nauckhoff and Adrian Del Caro (New York: Cambridge UP, 2001), 194.
3. Lisa Appignanesi, *Simone de Beauvoir* (London: Penguin, 1988), 137.

Appendix: Gathering the Stories

1. Hans-Georg Gadamer, *Truth and Method*, 2nd Revised ed., trans. Joel Weinsheimer and Donald G. Marshall (New York: Continuum, 2004), 295.
2. Martin Heidegger, *Being and Time*, trans. John Macquarrie and Edward Robinson (New York: Harper & Row, 1962), 24.

3. Ibid., 25.
4. Edmund Husserl, *The Crisis of the European Sciences and Transcendental Phenomenology*, trans. David Carr (Evanston: Northwestern University Press, 1970), 240.
5. Max Van Manen, *Researching Lived Experience: Human Science for an Action Sensitive Pedagogy* (New York: SUNY, 1997), 9.
6. Patricia Benner, *From Novice to Expert. Excellence and Power in Clinical Nursing Practice* (Menlo Park, CA: Addison-Wesley, 1984).
7. Alasdair MacIntyre, *After Virtue: A Study in Moral Theory* (Notre Dame: University of Notre Dame Press, 2007).
8. Christine Dinkins, "Shared Inquiry: Socratic-Hermeneutic Interpre-viewing," in *Beyond Method: Philosophical Conversations In Healthcare Research And Scholarship*, ed. Pamela M. Ironside (Madison: University of Wisconsin Press, 2005).
9. Hans-Georg Gadamer, *Truth and Method*, 2nd Revised ed., trans. Joel Weinsheimer and Donald G. Marshall (New York: Continuum, 2004), 369.
10. Martin Heidegger, *Discourse on Thinking*, trans. John M. Anderson and E. Hans Freund (New York: Harper & Row, 1966), 60.
11. Plato, *Euthyphro*, in *Five Dialogues*, 2nd ed., trans. G.M.A. Grube (Indianapolis: Hackett, 2002), 14b.
12. Hugh Benson, "The Priority of Definition and the Socratic *Elenchos*," in *Oxford Studies in Ancient Philosophy* 8 1990: 19–65.
13. Plato, *Theaetetus*, trans. M.J. Levett and Myles Burnyeat (Indianapolis: Hackett, 1990), 149b–150c.
14. Plato, *Republic*, trans. G.M.A. Grube and C.D.C. Reeve (Indianapolis: Hackett, 1992), Book VII.
15. Christine Dinkins, "Shared Inquiry: Socratic-Hermeneutic Interpre-viewing," in *Beyond Method: Philosophical Conversations In Healthcare Research And Scholarship*, ed. Pamela M. Ironside (Madison: University of Wisconsin Press, 2005), 141.
16. Hans-Georg Gadamer, *Truth and Method*, 2nd Revised ed., trans. Joel Weinsheimer and Donald G. Marshall (New York: Continuum, 2004), 379.

Bibliography

Appignanesi, Lisa. *Simone De Beauvoir*. London: Penguin, 1988.

Arendt, Hannah. "Labor, Work, Action." In *The Portable Hannah Arendt*, edited by Peter Baehr, 167–81. New York: Penguin Classics, 2003.

Bateson, Mary Catherine. *Full Circles, Overlapping Lives: Culture and Generation in Transition*. New York: Random House, 2000.

Benner, Patricia. *From Novice to Expert. Excellence and Power in Clinical Nursing Practice*. Menlo Park, CA: Addison-Wesley, 1984.

Benson, Hugh. "The Priority of Definition and the Socratic Elenchos." *Oxford Studies in Ancient Philosophy* 8 (1990): 19–65.

Carroll, Lewis. *Alice's Adventures in Wonderland*. Wellesley, MA: Branden Books, 1929.

Dinkins, Christine. "Shared Inquiry: Socratic-Hermeneutic Interpre-viewing." In *Beyond Method: Philosophical Conversations In Healthcare Research And Scholarship*, edited by Pamela M. Ironside, 111–47. Madison: University of Wisconsin Press, 2005.

Gadamer, Hans-Georg. *Truth and Method*. 2nd rev. ed. Translated by Joel Weinsheimer and Donald G. Marshall. New York: Continuum, 2004.

Gilligan, Carol. *In a Different Voice: Psychological Theory and Women's Development*. Cambridge, MA: Harvard University Press, 1982.

Heidegger, Martin. *Being and Time*. Translated by John Macquarrie and Edward Robinson. New York: Harper & Row, 1962.

———. *Discourse on Thinking*. Translated by John M. Anderson and E. Hans Freund. New York: Harper Torchbooks, 1969.

Heidegger, Martin. "The Nature of Language." In *On the Way to Language*, translated by Peter Hertz, 57–108. New York: Harper & Row, 1971.

Heraclitus, fragments. In *Readings in Ancient Greek Philosophy: From Thales to Aristotle*, 4th ed. Edited by S. Marc Cohen, Patricia Curd, and C.D.C. Reeve. Indianapolis: Hackett, 2011.

Husserl, Edmund. *The Crisis of the European Sciences and Transcendental Phenomenology*. Translated by David Carr. Evanston: Northwestern University Press, 1970.

Lopez, Barry. *Crow and Weasel*. San Francisco: North Point Press, 1990.

MacIntyre, Alasdair C. *After Virtue: A Study in Moral Theory*. Notre Dame: University of Notre Dame Press, 2007.

Nietzsche, Friedrich. *The Gay Science: With a Prelude in German Rhymes and an Appendix of Songs*. Edited by Bernard Williams. Translated by Josefine Nauckhoff and Adrian Del Caro. New York: Cambridge University Press, 2001.

———. *The Anti-Christ, Ecce Homo, Twilight of the Idols, And Other Writings*. Edited by Aaron Ridley. Translated by Judith Norman. New York: Cambridge University Press, 2005.

Plato. *Theaetetus*. Translated by M.J. Levett and Myles Burnyeat. Indianapolis: Hackett, 1990.

———. *Republic*. Translated by G.M.A. Grube and C.D.C. Reeve. Indianapolis: Hackett, 1992.

———. *Euthyphro*. In *Five Dialogues*, 2nd ed. Translated by G.M.A. Grube. Indianapolis: Hackett, 2002.

———. *Meno*. In *Five Dialogues*, 2nd ed. Translated by G.M.A. Grube. Indianapolis: Hackett, 2002.

Sartre, Jean-Paul. "Existentialism is a Humanism." In *Existentialism from Dostoyevsky to Sartre*, edited by Walter Kaufman and translated by Philip Mairet, 345–68. New York: Penguin, 1975.

Stein, Edith. *The Problem of Empathy*. 3rd rev. ed. Translated by Waltraut Stein. Washington, DC: ICS, 1989.

Van Manen, Max. *Researching Lived Experience: Human Science for an Action Sensitive Pedagogy*. New York: SUNY, 1997.

Whitehead, Alfred North. *Process and Reality: An Essay in Cosmology*. New York: The Free Press, 1982.

Index

Note: *To help preserve anonymity, pseudonyms of research participants have not been indexed.*

advisor
 being friends with 115–16
 best practices of 110, 120–2, 135, 174
 choosing 106
 conflicts with 51, 76, 114, 170
 as diplomat 109–11, 123, 127–8, 155
 evolving relationship with 98, 134
 experienced vs. inexperienced 109–10, 147, 149, 155
 recognizing her/his support after the fact 134, 142
 understanding communication style 85, 114, 116, 118, 124, 133
 working long-distance with 118–19
 see also communication with advisor
advisor's office 88–9, 124
advisor–student relationship
 ideal 107–9, 111, 114, 119
 real 114, 117, 119, 129
Alice in Wonderland 15, 17
alienation 52, 69, 92
alone
 feeling x, 39, 42, 64, 92
 working 38–9, 41, 86, 114, 154

anxiety 90, 101, 119, 141, 155
 after completion 169
aporia 186–7
Arendt, Hannah 137
authenticity 4–5, 16, 186

balance, finding 48, 65, 77–8, 91–2, 95
barriers 70, 95, 141
Bateson, Mary Catherine 71, 99
Beauvoir, Simone de 176
big picture 10, 26, 35, 46
books, dissertation
 how-to 19–20
boss 66–7

capabilities 94, 97, 166
career
 dissertation's place in 11, 83, 91, 159, 175
 pursuing degree to advance 45, 83, 134–5
caring 131, 135
chair, *see* advisor
challenges 19, 130, 176, 179
children 12, 52, 59, 62, 73, 77–8, 91–5, 101, 141
 caring for 48–9, 52
 pressure to have 58, 60
 support from 61–2, 73, 172
 see also daughters; sons

cliff, like jumping off a 27–8
co-inquirers 159, 180–1,
    184–5; *see also* shared
    inquiry
colleagues at workplace 32, 39,
    63, 66, 68
commitment 3, 27, 165–6, 187
committee members
    choosing 104–8, 110
    as co-inquirers 157–8
    differing views among 126–7
    difficult 67, 109–10, 128–30,
        148–52
    seeking help from
        individual 119
communication with advisor
    high-stakes vs. low-stakes
        32, 108
    ideal 32, 108
    via email 67, 110, 113,
        118–19, 132–3
    see also feedback
competency, demonstrating
    2, 7–8
confidence
    from committee 131–2
    faking 87
    increase in 21, 173
    lack of 29, 36, 85–9
    self- 60, 75, 86, 89, 116
    in writing abilities 33, 82
confusion 19–21, 43, 46,
    55, 125
    positive outcomes from 41
contamination of home
    and family 49–50, 95
conversations
    about dissertation 17
    with advisor and committee
        17, 119, 138, 158
    changed nature of 48, 69, 71
    with friends 53
    with husband 49

coursework, transition from 21,
    27–31, 33, 46, 86
co-workers, *see* colleagues
credibility from PhD work 9–10

daughters 57–8, 62, 93–4
deadlines 62, 85, 117
defense
    as blur 151–2
    as coronation 140–2,
        150–1, 155
    as fun 146, 152–3
    as fusion of horizons 156–8
    as rite of passage 140, 146
    as shared inquiry 158–9
    being the expert during 143–4,
        154, 158–9
    cancelled 139, 147
    chair's role in 109, 139,
        141–3, 147, 149–51, 155
    family present for 141–2
    friends present for 145–6
    preparing for 134, 141, 145,
        155, 159
    problems during 148–50
    public 142, 146
    reactions to completion
        of 146, 154, 167
depression 39
despair 39, 83, 85
development, self- 5, 96, 136
discovery 3, 43, 89
    excitement of 43
dissertation
    as exercise 2–3, 12, 35
    as hoop to jump through
        2, 11, 13, 15–16, 18
    as job 29, 97
    as leap 21, 27–8, 33, 44
    as refuge 55
    as rite of passage 11–13
    in context of life's work
        10, 23, 90

dissertation experience
  ideal 186
  like pregnancy 4
dissertations as guides,
  others' 17, 98
distractions 33, 37, 70, 78
divorce 54
drafts 26, 31, 113, 118, 138

email, *see* communication with
  advisor, via email
emotional aftereffects from
  dissertation 162, 170
emotions 53, 94, 100, 173
empathy 101, 147
existentialism 99–100, 176
expertise
  from committee members
    106, 111, 154
  demonstrating in defense
    143–4, 154, 158–9
  dissertation as path to 8–10,
    86, 96, 134

failures, perceived 65, 171, 176
family
  caring for 52, 78, 94, 112
  changed relationship with
    71, 94
  lack of support from 56
  negative effects on 50, 95
  present for defense 141–2
  support from 56–7, 59, 62
  see also under individual
    members
father 59, 61, 92, 146
fear 27, 69, 88, 96, 147
feedback
  helpful 33, 66, 81, 128, 164
  lack of helpful 30, 33,
    113, 126
  negative 51, 87, 134
  positive 116, 132

  problems caused by 37, 87, 116
  seeking outside 32–3, 66, 82
  timeliness of 24, 30–1
forgiveness 137
fragility of doctoral students
  87, 128
freedom 16, 41
friends, women 53, 63–4, 69
friendships
  best 71
  maintaining 52, 116
  transformation in 72
frustration 128, 130
fun
  in defense 146, 152–3
  in dissertation process 57, 80,
    146, 170
  inability to have 72, 79
fusion of horizons 156–8

Gadamer, Hans-Georg 156–8,
  181–3, 186, 188
gender differences x–xi, 62,
  70–1
gender roles 54–5, 91
Gilligan, Carol 70
grandmother 60
growth
  intellectual 9, 21, 156
  personal 16, 71
guilt 40, 113

Heidegger, Martin 44–5, 158,
  181–3
Heraclitus 155
hermeneutics 156–7, 181,
  183, 188
  hermeneutic circle 186–7
household responsibilities
  48, 50, 54, 56, 73,
  91, 95
  dinner 49–50, 54, 56
hurt 113, 118, 128, 137

husband
  divorced during doctoral work 54
  emotional support from 37, 49–51, 141–2, 173
  lack of support from 49, 56, 62
  sharing household chores 50, 91
  see also partner
Husserl, Edmund 182

ideals, value of reflecting on 185–6
impostor syndrome 6, 84, 87, 100–1
independence, expected new level of 33, 42
intimidation 17, 29, 88–9
isolation xi, 21, 38, 41, 46, 138
  positive outcomes from 41

job, *see* workplace
job market 115, 170
joys 38, 135, 176

language style in dissertation 29, 148
leap into the unknown 21, 27–8, 30, 33, 44, 46, 100
learning from dissertation process 7, 12, 96–7, 99, 111, 186
lessons 22, 42–3, 172
letdown after completion 168, 170
life
  as distraction 33, 35, 70, 111
  as existentialist journey 176
  effect of dissertation on 36, 40, 75, 92, 95, 163, 169
lived experience 180–3
loneliness 30, 39, 176
  loneliest loneliness 175–6

Lopez, Barry xii
lost
  causes for feeling 6, 27, 33–4, 44, 127
  feeling 33–4, 43, 45
  overcoming feeling 37

MacIntyre, Alasdair xi
Master's thesis 4, 78
Meno's paradox 15–16
mentors 117, 119–20, 132
midwifing-of-ideas 184–5
mother, student's role as 50, 56–7, 91, 94
  single mother 62
mother of student 56, 58–9, 80, 169
  as cheerleader 59, 70, 169
Myers-Briggs 30
mystery 19–21, 24, 27, 33, 46, 104
  openness to the 44–5
  positive aspects of 41, 43

Nietzsche, Friedrich 175–6
novice in scholarly research 5, 144

obsessing 89, 91
office, *see* workspace for writing
originality of dissertation 2, 6, 16, 18
ownership of dissertation, personal 3–4, 6, 16, 125

panicking 163, 167
parents 58–9
partner 48–9, 52
  afraid of alienating 69
  supportive but impatient 51
  see also husband
peer group, lack of consistent 39–40

peers
  comparing oneself to 98
  competition among 68
  lack of support from 39
  seeking feedback from 32
  support from 17–18, 39, 116
planning 44–5, 77, 91, 112, 187
Plato 183
possibilities xi, 72–3, 100
post-doctoral research 144, 170
power 36, 88–9, 100
pressure 62, 84, 91–4
pride 11, 25, 172–3
process-relational philosophy 72
progress 65, 109, 121, 123
  lack of 34, 36, 109, 125
promises 32, 137–8
proposal, dissertation 14, 25, 31, 93, 125, 166
PTSD from dissertation process 170

quality
  assessing 26, 85
  desire for 56, 66, 164
  of writing 29
quit
  come too far to 59, 77, 129
  temptation to 24, 59, 67, 108, 125, 165

realizations 54, 90, 92, 100, 155
relationship with advisor, *see* advisor–student relationship
relax, difficult to 40, 84
research participants for dissertation 5, 82, 186
resentment 54, 94, 135
responsibilities, household, *see* household responsibilities
rewrites 12, 29, 62, 150

rite of passage
  defense as 140, 146
  dissertation as 11–13

Sartre, Jean-Paul 100
scholar, self as 6, 100–1, 156, 159
scholarship 72, 83–4, 156
self-confidence 60, 75, 86, 89, 116; *see also* confidence
self-direction 31, 41–2
self-doubt, *see* impostor syndrome
self-esteem 87
self-perceptions 100–1
shared inquiry x, 17–18, 158–9, 188; *see also* co-inquirers
shooting range, taking dissertation to 131
sisters 57–8
skills
  developing new 28–9, 46, 57, 81
  interpersonal 82, 102
  writing 33, 127
sleep, need for 92, 95, 153
Socrates 15–16, 183–5, 187
sons 49, 61–2, 70, 78–9, 94, 141
Stein, Edith 100–1
steps of dissertation process
  not communicated well by program 21, 24–6, 42, 123
  not the issue 27
  lack of big picture 26
stories, value of sharing x–xii, 20, 182–3, 188
strengths, knowing weaknesses and 29, 79–80, 82
stress 34, 37, 98, 107, 133
  of balancing priorities 91
  coping methods 51, 63, 95
  as positive force 56
structure of a dissertation 8, 28

stuck
  causes of becoming   34–7, 88, 108
  overcoming being   37, 46, 63
  as vicious cycle   36
  see also writer's block
support group   63–5, 114
  online   64

tediousness of the process   23, 55
thinking
  calculative   44–5
  critical   10–11
  meditative   44–5
timeline   25, 78–9, 122, 138
too-many-cooks problem   126–7
topic, choosing a   22–3, 30, 45

unknown territory   21, 44, 136, 138, 155
unpredictability of human interaction   137

vagueness   15–16
validation   29, 51, 68, 85, 92, 186
  lack of   87, 91
venting   37, 46
video chat, working by   64
vulnerability   112, 127, 135, 138, 176

weaknesses, knowing strengths and   29, 79–80, 82
Whitehead, Alfred North   72
women as support   63–5, 70
workplace   32, 36, 43, 67, 166
workplace supervisor   66–7
workspace for writing   49, 58, 62, 78, 80
worry   35, 48, 69; *see also* fear
worthy   81–2, 99
writer's block   21, 34, 88; *see also* stuck

GPSR Compliance

The European Union's (EU) General Product Safety Regulation (GPSR) is a set of rules that requires consumer products to be safe and our obligations to ensure this.

If you have any concerns about our products, you can contact us on

ProductSafety@springernature.com

In case Publisher is established outside the EU, the EU authorized representative is:

Springer Nature Customer Service Center GmbH
Europaplatz 3
69115 Heidelberg, Germany

www.ingramcontent.com/pod-product-compliance
Lightning Source LLC
LaVergne TN
LVHW020345260326
834688LV00045B/1537